Soar with Vulnerability

Eleven Insights to the Full

Enjoyment of Your Life

Suzanne Letourneau

Published by Skye Insights Company

Copyrights © 2012 by Suzanne Letourneau
301 Carlissa Run
Newmarket, ON L3X 3G9

Editorial supervision: Cliff Carl
Design: Just Ink Digital Design

No part of this publication may be reproduced or transmitted in any form or by any means, mechanical or electronic, including photocopying and recording, or by any information storage and retrieval system, without permission in writing from author or publisher (except by a reviewer, who may quote brief passages and/or show brief video clips in a review).

SOAR WITH VULNERABILITY — ELEVEN

INSIGHTS TO THE FULL ENJOYMENT OF YOUR

LIFE

ISBN 978-0-9859538-8-1

DEDICATION

To *Stan*, my partner in life, for being there at all times, even when I was not.

TABLE OF CONTENTS

Preface i

Introduction v

How To Read This Book ix

Chapter One: Beginnings 13

Chapter Two: Survival 19

Chapter Three: Closing Doors 29

Chapter Four: Finding My Purpose 35

Chapter Five: Insight 1 — Vulnerability 45

Chapter Six: Insight 2 — Surrender 55

Chapter Seven: Insight 3 — Pain 61

Chapter Eight: Insight 4 — Authenticity ... 73

Chapter Nine: Insight 5 — Conscious

    Awareness 85

Chapter Ten: Insight 6 — Clarity 93

Chapter Eleven: Insight 7 — Passion 103

Chapter Twelve: Insight 8 — Meaningful 107

Chapter Thirteen: Insight 9 — Emptiness 115

Chapter Fourteen: Insight 10 — Freedom 121

Chapter Fifteen: Insight 11 — Alive &
   Soaring 131

The Ego Releasing Chart 137

PREFACE

Cherish your visions and dreams as they are the children of your soul,
the blueprints of your ultimate achievements
Napoleon Hill.

I cherished every second, every moment of my dream until June of 2004, when my soul lost its child; this child was my life's purpose. It had a name, a vision, a plan. It was my company, my self-created business. And I had just lost it all. For me it felt the same as losing a child. A child that was inspiring to all who touched it, a child born with the gift of healing; a child that brought comfort to all by making a positive difference in their lives. And how many lives we have comforted! Hundreds and hundreds! My business was an oxygen wellness airport spa located in just a few airports, with the vision to be located in all major hub airports in the world.

Suddenly and abruptly, I lost everything to my

investors. Because of a lack of common vision, my lack of acumen, negotiating skills, the hidden agenda of my investors and God knows what else; the rug got pulled right out from under me. What the heck had just happened? By mysterious ways, I was forced out of my own company, the company I had founded through love and faith.

This sent me into a sinking spiral where I found myself with no purpose, no passion, and no excitement for life. I had lost the dream that more people than just I had put hopes in. Could I count on my best friend that had served me well in the past, my **invulnerability**?

So I thought. But this time it was different. I felt guilty for having failed the ones that trusted in me the most. I was a failure and I was helpless. Along with everything else there went my self-esteem, my self-worth, my 'joie de vivre'. Not knowing what my purpose was anymore, I just started floating through life aimlessly.

For five long years, I kept on floating, kept on trying, pretending that I was not hurt, that everything was okay, hiding my vulnerability; the one thing I knew I could do very well. In 2009, while I was attending yet another training seminar, I found myself in front of a group of people with a microphone in my hand. How had that happened? I have no clue. In all the other seminars or conferences I'd attended I made sure I was invisible in the room. This time all I knew was that it felt so familiar standing there, humble and defenseless, with a microphone, just like riding a bicycle. My whole being turned inward and I felt something happening.

For the first time in five excruciating years, I could actually feel something. ***Could something still be alive inside of me?***

Up to that point I had been lifeless but now I could sense that something was beginning to percolate. I started to feel more sensitive and more real than ever before.

From this unexpected feeling of aliveness I heard a little voice talking to me: *You are not dead and you are not a failure. You have never been and never will be a failure. There is no such thing as failure. You are a passionate complete being.*

Suzanne Letourneau

I brought the microphone closer to my face and started talking. I started sharing my newly discovered *Vulnerability*

INTRODUCTION

Before I continue with vulnerability or share the other insights I have received or learned, I feel it is important for you to know where I come from. What makes me the authority on the subject? Why am I writing this book on vulnerability?

We all have a story to tell and your story is probably not vastly different than mine. One difference perhaps is that I have decided to write about it in order to heal myself from a pain so deep that *the only way out of it, is in*. To go inside of me and rediscover my greatness. As you can imagine this is not an easy task. This might actually be one of the most difficult things I ever did in my life. Jumping out of an airplane at 13,000 feet is exciting; but allowing myself to be totally and completely vulnerable, and further writing about it, that is terrifying.

I have never before written a book or even

imagined I would. In writing this book I want to inspire you to go beyond the façade of who you think you are.

Why this book now? Because the biggest turning point of my life has opened my heart to receiving the biggest gift of all – Vulnerability. Because it is time for me to *Embrace my Vulnerability openly and freely,* and help others do the same.

In the first insight I will share the *secret power* of vulnerability and all the other treasures it brings along. Right now you might think that it sounds crazy, but once we complete this journey together, you will realize at a deep level how this is "home" to you, and to all of us. The road to bring you back home is right there in front of you.

I will share some very private information about my life, not out of ego but from my heart. This way you'll know where I come from, what I have accomplished or not, some of my challenges and fears. You'll also know that I am writing this book to complete my own healing, to help you with yours, and this is only the beginning of what is possible to accomplish.

I felt that in order for this book to have a

positive impact on your life, I needed to find different ways to connect with each and every one of you. Some of you might connect with my childhood traumas and others with my ongoing journey to find the meaning of life. Some of you will connect to the entrepreneurship and others to the power of a down point in your life. Whatever it is, I invite you to let yourself find yourself in me as I have found myself in others like you.

We are One but we are all Unique in our Beingness and Mission on this planet.

There were many situations that I was reluctant or hesitant to share; you will surely identify them. I trust that all the details given will help you relate to your own experiences, look at them from a different perspective, and grow from it. I encourage you to start writing your own story as you read mine. Take notes, stop and feel, close your eyes, experience your own energy and discover your own insights. Now more than ever it is time to realize how connected we are. This is your book. The book that is inside of you *all-ways*. Let it shine.

Later, I will reveal the *Eleven Insights* that will guide you through your transformation into the full enjoyment of your life.

Personally, I called them *Insights From Freedom*, for they helped me break free from my limiting ego. I needed to experience each insight, and make sure that every one of them was coming from a place of true clarity and authenticity — my soul core.

In turn, a whole new exciting life, and ultimate feeling of true freedom, is also waiting for you.

HOW TO READ THIS BOOK

Soar with Vulnerability is the result of my emotional roller coaster and the resulting experiences gathered throughout my life. Further-more it is a summary of my life's research; all the books, all the seminars, and all the trainings I've been through during those agonizing five years, and much beyond that.

I love books. I read them, process them and reread them again many years later. I always get a new understanding or a new enlightenment from it.

I found out why most self-help books are basically teaching the same thing. It is because they all borrow from each other. As one, we all feed on each other. One sharing becomes the inspiration for another. And that other becomes the inspiration of another one. And so on. But for some reason certain books resonate with you much stronger than others.

Suzanne Letourneau

Please allow your heart, not your mind, to read this book. Your eyes will see the letters, the pictures and all, but your heart will read, will feel, offering you a liberating experience. After each and every insight I suggest you take the time to close your eyes and be with your own particular experiences, feelings and emotions that wish to be healed.

Where does each insight take you? What realization have you made through it? We all have mixed emotions, each and every day, towards and for so many different things. Emotions are there to bring you closer to who you really are. Our thoughts, our words, and our actions create our emotions and the world we live in. All these emotions and challenges are all intertwined and connected like the luminous strands of the Universe.

My intention is not to teach you or lecture you. My intention is to share what I have learned and discovered from each and every one of the emotions, negative and positive, I have experienced; to help you reconnect with your divinity, and to inspire you to make a difference in your life.

The purpose of this book is to Inspire. Inspire

you to be the spirit that you are, to go for your heart's vision, your calling. To reconnect to whom you really are.

I invite you to join me in this wonderful adventure to experience, to live, and to be. And ultimately to "remember" that you are Inspiration.

CHAPTER ONE

Beginnings

So where do I come from? I am the middle child of a family of three girls from middle class working parents in Montreal, QC. My mom was the manager of a bowling alley, working at night. My dad worked during the day as a security guard first, then as electrician for an industrial company in downtown Montreal. Dad was also the janitor of five apartment buildings, at night and on week-ends; that is if and when he was home. We lived in one of these buildings. Often my sisters and I had to fill in for my dad, doing his janitorial duties. This was quite a challenge.

In those years we had to burn the garbage that had been thrown down the chute from all the apartments. Of course some of the garbage could not be burned, such as bottles. So my younger sister and I had to sort through it all, and take the trash that would burn and throw it into the incinerator. Not an easy task for little girls. I remember my older sister washing the walls, the stairs handrail, and windows in the buildings.

My dad was suffering from alcoholism, disappearing for days at a time. When he would finally show up, we never knew what to expect. Often there was no paycheck for weeks. On payday he might have decided to join his buddies at the tavern. By the time he would make it back home the paycheck was already consumed.

Very unpleasant were the many times we had to go and drag our dad out of the tavern and bring him back home. When my father was under the influence of alcohol there were always arguments, yelling and fighting with my mother, his brothers or other adults who were around. There was always lots of screaming, tears, cries and the fear of who might get hurt — including myself.

I recall helping my mother clean the blood from my father's face after a fight with his brother; a policeman ringing at our door because a neighbor complained; or having to rush to the hospital emergency.

My two sisters and I would hide in our room

when we heard him coming in late at night. And when he would ask in a gruff voice: "Which one of my little girls will cook me something to eat?" one of us would get up, most often I did, pretending that I was strong and nothing would happen. After all he was my father. In an eight-year-old mind, it was a big step to face your fear and do it anyway.

I had no real reason to be afraid of him; he never touched me, or hurt me. He was a very loving father when sober. I have lots of fond memories, like swimming across a mile long lake beside him. Catching chipmunks just for the fun of watching them and feeding them for a while, before releasing them back into the wild. Or learning how to apply mud on my skin after a wasp sting.

In the earlier years when my mother was not working yet, she went through the neighbor's garbage to find us new clothes. My older sister was extremely embarrassed one day when the girl from across the street recognized her own clothes on my sister.

As the middle child I rarely got new clothes. I had to wear my older sister's clothes, or the other people's clothes that my sister had worn, before passing them on to my younger sister; that is if the clothes were still in condition to be worn.

When my mother started working, she had to perform miracles with her small paycheck to feed and clothe us. Nevertheless, I don't ever remember going hungry. Mother was somewhat creative with her recipes and the leftovers. I do remember a lot of beans, sheppard pies, and pea soup.

I also remember a very different type of "treats" at my paternal grandfather's house. You see, even though my father wasn't home a lot, and rarely talked about his father, my mother insisted that we'd go and visit our grandfather. Maybe she wanted to be a good parent, showing us by example that every child should have a chance to meet their grandfather. Maybe she wanted some type of support? Or maybe, it was just her way to take us out for an inexpensive Sunday afternoon? Unfortunately, once again, this turned out to be another unpleasant experience for my sisters and me.

My grandfather had moved into a small shack on one of the poorest streets of downtown Montreal, in St. Henry. He had left his wife and thirteen children many years ago, and was living with this grossly overweight Aboriginal woman. I remember their place being dirty and smelly. We were always reluctant to go in and kiss him on the cheek and all. But then for some unexplainable reason, when it was time to leave, we didn't want to go. We wanted to stay a while longer, and hear more stories, and laugh a little more. It was always with sadness that we left. It took me some time to understand that I did not love or hate my grand-father. I just did not know him. He had dis-appeared from dad's life at an early age, therefore he had also been out of mine. How do all those pieces come back together? One day I will understand.

My younger sister and I were physically abused by our maternal grandfather. I remember the day and the moment. One of my uncles and his wife would rent this little cottage over the summer where we would sometimes go to be with family. We'd play with ours cousins, swim in the lake, and for one rare moment have a normal child's life. It was in the car on the way back from one visit at the cottage that it happened.

We had to squeeze everybody into one small

car. So my younger sister and I would end up sitting on my grandfather's lap. That particular day, my grandfather somehow thought it would be okay to start feeling us, touching our private parts over our bathing suits. When you are six and seven years old you just don't know how to react to those things. We just looked at each other, felt each other's fear, and said nothing.

Later on I was physically abused by the baby sitter. Not the same kind of abuse. The kind that hurts you differently. "If you don't do as I say …" and suddenly her long fingers nails would dig into my arm. As soon as I could get away, I'd run, and glue myself to the wall under the bunk beds.

I started working when I was ten years old, babysitting for people in the building. Then at age eleven I worked in an amusement park hustling at a pitch toss game. At twelve years old I took a job flipping burgers and making club sandwiches at the bowling alley where my mother was the manager.

That's where I was the day we received an upsetting phone call.

CHAPTER TWO

Survival

My father had disappeared. Again, Dad's disappearance was not an unusual event. Dad was known to take off for days at a time and then just show up, acting as if nothing had happened and this was all perfectly normal. This time he had "gone fishing" with some guys, and he never came back. It was the police who found him two days later. That was the phone call.

He was dead. Dad had drowned! Drowned? My dad was a great swimmer. How could that be? We couldn't believe what we were hearing. And then the case was promptly classified as a "no case". There would be no further investigation into whether or not my father had been "assisted" into the water.

And so my father was gone forever; his death shrouded in mystery. That was the reality. I was only thirteen years old. Thirteen but *heroically invulnerable.*

***

How is it so far? Does your story sound a little like mine? Or perhaps you had it even harder than I did, and my story sounds a little tepid to you by comparison. Nevertheless, if you keep on reading I guarantee that the insights I am about to share with you will definitely help make a difference in your life as well.

From a very young age, because of all the embarrassments and fears I have been through, I've learned to hide my vulnerability and act strong. I've learned to hide my shame and my humiliation. I understood the importance of being strong and the meaning of survival. That's when I created a shield of emotional protection by making myself heroically *invulnerable*; and invulnerable I was for over forty years.

I believed that by being invulnerable, nobody would be able to hurt me or see what was really going on inside of me. I was very young but I felt I was what they call an "old soul". In the hope of realizing my all-time dream of "making a positive impact in this world", I created my own type of "survival kit". My *survival kit* was basically a ritual. I would go to this hiding place, usually under the steps of one of the staircases of the apartment building, where I would try to hold back my tears and hide my hurt. But then of course the hurt would always get to be too much and I would cry; I would let it all out where nobody would see me or hear me. When I had no more tears left, and felt my heart calmer, I would come out of my hiding place, all pumped up and more determined than ever to succeed without asking anyone for anything. Pretending that I was okay, that I could not be hurt, and that I was once again completely invulnerable.

Growing up I never had, neither from my mother or father, any encouragement in believing in myself. Never got a pat on the back for the good stuff I had done or any discussions on the limitless opportunities that lay in front of me. Everyone was concerned with their own survival. When my father died, I started living in a different type of fear. Fear of not knowing what path to take to get on the road to success. My mother kept on encouraging me to become a secretary or a teacher.

Suzanne Letourneau

I wanted to be an interpreter and travel the world meeting people from different countries. Today I understand that they raised me to the best of their capabilities, and that they only had as tools the way that they had been raised themselves.

All the same, every "punch" of indifference, of ignorance or non-encouragement that was thrown at me, became a source of inspiration to move to higher levels of connection of who I was, and my purpose of being here on Earth. I always kept on going, hiding my fears, hiding my pain, and breaking down new walls. Nothing was going to stop me from succeeding and making a difference with my life. What I did not know was that this invulnerability and my determination to make a positive difference in people's lives would be necessary to get me through several stages of my life.

At age seventeen I went on to work at a cable TV station learning the on-air procedures; plus I worked in disco bars as a barmaid and as a DJ. Not always the safest ones. One night when working as a DJ at Yesterday's Club in Montreal, I heard a loud BANG! then I saw my dance floor emptying in less than ten seconds. Someone had just shot somebody with a shotgun. The shot could have come from anywhere; with loud disco music playing it was hard to tell. There was a moment of petrified silence, then screaming and the start of panic. Soon we all heard muffled sounds of fighting from one particular corner. The villain was caught...and life must go on; so I cued up "Let the Music Play" by Shannon.

***

I kept my challenging night jobs, but moved on to include being a model and TV co-host on a popular variety show on TVA-TV, "Disco Tourne". It was the high time of disco music. On air, I got to mingle with the disco stars of the day, such as the Village People, Tina Charles, Gloria Gaynor, Vicky Sue Robinson, George McCrae, Bonnie M, Ogie, and more. I even got to personally meet with the legend superstar Mr. James Brown. I still have a picture of me kissing him on the cheek. This was one of the most exciting times of my life.

When the opportunity presented itself to travel the world, quit the night jobs and create some type of long term security in my life, I jumped at the offer to become a flight attendant with Air Canada. And in my off hours I trained and became a Certified Personal Trainer.

Had I reached my dream of making a positive impact in people's lives? Obviously not as I did not feel fulfilled, did not feel the passion. Being a dependable flight attendant was important but certainly not my purpose in life. So what was my calling? What was my mission? I had to find out! Hence I broke another wall.

This wall was daring to take a whole year leave of absence from the airlines and moving to the beautiful island of Barbados, West Indies.

Living in Barbados and going to Barbados for the ideal vacation, are two completely different things. I was entirely on my own with no family or friends around me. I became one of the natives, had to make a living, and experience the island life challenges. Finding the money to pay my rent or having a decent meal was often an issue. So I had to be creative! I took a job on the Jolly Roger "pirate boat", selling key chain pictures to the drunken tourists as well as bartending at different beach bars. But still this was not enough to adequately eat and pay my rent.

I was a Certified Aerobic Instructor & Personal Trainer, so I started teaching at different fitness clubs on the island, building a name for myself, even though I wasn't legally allowed to work. My big break came when I met a wonderful lady, Maureen Branson, owner of the Fitness & Spa Center at the Hilton hotel. She had heard about me and asked me to join her company to train her instructors and run the fitness part of the business. She applied for my work permit and I found myself legally getting paid doing something I loved to do: teaching and training.

Nevertheless, I still had to face my inner fears, my beliefs, my values, myself. *When and where in my life am I living my true spirit? Who am I and why am I here?*

I felt my spiritual self transported by the sound of each wave and the gentle touch of the wind; my skin receiving the warm caresses of the sun. I embraced the nostalgic and inspiring mystery of the ocean, and opened myself to its message. And there it was. A bigger sense of contribution was calling to me. It was time to close this chapter of my life and start a new one.

***

After not one year, but five enlightening years on the island, I returned to my job as a flight attendant and simultaneously accepted the position of "Spa Director" at a famous Five Star Relais & Chateaux Resort in ON, Canada, "The Inn at Manitou".

So here I was on the plane on my way back to Canada. Leaving my humble modest beach house and bohemian lifestyle behind to discover the lifestyle of the rich and famous. I was crying; crying in gratitude and hopefulness.

The Inn at Manitou was like a small island on its own. As all gems are, it was well hidden in the beautiful Georgian Bay Highlands. People from all around the world came to work here, as it was a privileged thing to have on your resume. And people from all around the world came to the Inn to spend an expensive, luxurious weekend of pampering, playing tennis, eating fancy gourmet foods and tasting the most refined wines.

During my first season at the Inn, I learned

about the Ego. Being trapped on a small island with not too many places to hide, the egos started showing up readily; either from my coworkers, my staff, or the Inn's guests.

One incident concerned a senior massage therapist. I say *senior* because some staff members were quite a bit older than I was. Or so it stated on their application.

This particular massage therapist had lots of difficulties taking orders or directions from me, the Spa Director. She would question or resist each one of my request and encourage the rest of the staff to follow her lead. Being the oldest, she pretended to be the wisest: "I've done this, done that, I know this, I know that," etc. Fortunately it didn't take me long to realize that her actions were all Ego driven. As a result, I became determined to not let myself be in my ego.

That's when I discovered the book *A Course in Miracles*. I have read many books in my life but none that had the clarity, the depth and the uniqueness of this one. This course has taught me so many things and has helped me undo old teachings and beliefs that no longer served me. One of the insights that I will share with you, further in the book, comes from the life lessons I have received through the course.

All my spare moments and many of my layovers as a flight attendant were spent studying that book, the 365 awakening lessons. My first season at the Inn was one of "re-self-discovery".

Self-discovery and introspection are seldom easy, and more often very difficult to accomplish. The *Ego* is always in the way of our true self, showing us the things that it wants us to believe. But I dug and I dug, until I acknowledged to myself beyond the *Ego*. I had not been living my truth. *I was still not living my purpose in life.*

Therefore at the end of the season at the Inn at Manitou, I made a commitment to myself – *to engage only in the things that would take me closer to my life's purpose.*

CHAPTER THREE

Closing Doors

In order to get closer to my life's purpose I knew I had to close some old doors and open new ones. So first, I decided to go back to Montreal, my hometown, to end the relationship with my longtime boyfriend. This relationship had been dragging on for years. It was not helping him or me in being or living our true destiny. It was very difficult to do of course. Because even though I did not *love* him in the same loving way, I still felt love for him.

The second thing was to do everything I could to make my vision come true. *Let's break another wall.* So I got my transfer with the airlines to fly out of Toronto instead of Montreal; moved to Toronto and opened my own wellness center, *Letourneau & Associates, Lifestyle & Fitness Center*.

I certainly did not have any money to pay for marketing research, design, renovation, etc. But one thing I had for sure was determination and a clear vision of wanting to make a real difference. With Stan's support, the new man in my life, and the help of one couple, Cathy & Perry Dolente, who I had met at the Inn, I was able to find some space and create my holistic fitness center. The mission of the center was to help each and every one understand themselves holistically: Body, Mind, and Spirit.

My center offered fitness classes, personal training, seminars, workshops, Tai Chi classes, Chi gong, massage therapy, shiatsu; and had a small bookstore. And of course weekly meetings on *A Course in Miracles*, facilitated by a wonderful spirit, Paul Cestnick. Priceless! I kept on learning from the course and sharing it with others.

We also invited special guest speakers for an evening or weekend seminar, such as Paul Ferrini, author of *The Silence of the Heart*, *Return to the Garden* and many more great books. Paul's work is heart-centered, empowering each and every one of us to move through our fear, and share who we are authentically.

I discovered the true meaning of unconditional

Soar With Vulnerability

love in swimming with wild dolphins in the open ocean. This was the "Rebirthing" time as I like to call it. Rebirthing is about *Conscious Energy Breathing* which is the most natural healing ability of all. How is it connected to the dolphins? The dolphins have conscious breathing versus us humans, where we don't even think about it. You can learn more about it in the book *Rebirthing*, by Leonard Orr and Sandra Ray.

Through the Center I was finally starting to make some difference in people's lives. All this holistic teaching was new to a lot of people, but not to me. I had been researching, reading, and investigating all of my life, on one's purpose in life and the balance of mind, body, and spirit.

In order to support the Center financially I had to keep my position at Air Canada, and my second year contract at the Inn at Manitou. Now I was spending my time between flying with Air Canada from Sunday nights to Tuesday afternoon. Landing at Toronto Pearson Airport on Tuesdays around three o'clock and rushing to my center to teach the 5:30 PM class. I would then spend the next two days working at my center before I had to leave for the Inn again on Thursday afternoon. Each drive to the Inn was three hours.

It would then start all over again on Sunday afternoon where I would need to leave the Inn to go back to the airport. On Sundays this drive could be a lot more, because of all the people coming back from their cottages.

Six long months of commuting between three commitments. The sense of being on a mission and my determination of making a difference got me through it.

The day my contract ended at the Inn, I was able to focus on the growth of the Center. I started my days with Personal Training sessions at 7:00 AM and closed the Center at 9:00 PM. That is if I didn't have any workshop/seminars planned for that evening. I worked twelve to fourteen hours a day, six days a week, for two years.

Unfortunately, after three years of struggling to make it through, interlocking with wonderful and beautiful miracles, I had to make the decision to close the Center before it totally drowned me. I worked up my courage, called upon my *invulnerability*, gathered my members, and shared my concerns with them. After a sharing of tears and emotions, I also informed them that I was going to facilitate a study group on *A Course in Miracles* from my home for whoever might be interested. And so the small miracles kept on happening! I would keep on looking for a more appropriate location for the Center to reopen.

One day I was stuck at the airport with four hours between flights — I was deeply concerned and disturbed by the waste of time with nothing to do — and certainly nothing healthy. In that moment I had an epiphany!

CHAPTER FOUR

Finding My Purpose

The seeds of a new business concept began to germinate and I suddenly became an entrepreneur. A real entrepreneur, who had understood the pain of a need. An entrepreneur, who had found her true passion, her life's purpose. This was going to be the location of my ultimate project. I started working tenaciously to bring my vision to reality; this was 1996.

I knew this time I had to do it right. Do a market research, make a business plan, do some financial assumptions, do a lot of research & development and simultaneously approach potential investors and airport management.

Talk about breaking walls down!

I worked my way through government owned airports, banks, airport's authority red tape, requests for proposal processes, venture capitalist or may I say "vulture capitalists" and my lack of knowledge in the big financial world. The process sped up my growth in the business world and probably gave me my first grey hair. At the same time I was working on the creation of the brand; skin care, herbal vitamins for jet-lag and fatigue, aromatherapy, etc.

I worked with designers to create a unique design for my first location, the staff's uniforms, and finding reliable local suppliers. Everything had to be in place before I would finally get a yes from someone.

In 2000, after four long years of hard work, research & development, deceptions and frustrations, I finally succeeded in finding investors to support my vision:

The creation of OraOxygen. The first Oxygen Wellness Airport Spa in the world and it has emerged as the biggest novelty.

Mission Statement

"To globally provide all air travelers, airline and airport employees with unique and specialized

Soar With Vulnerability

products & services that focus on physical, mental, and spiritual wellness."

This would make a positive difference in people's lives. This was going to make a positive diffcrence in my life. I was finally living my dream, my vision, and my passion. After working so hard all my life, I had finally made it out of the "rat race". There would be no more hurts and no more embarrassments.

I remember wonderful precious moments. When people got stranded at the airport because of a snowstorm or an extended flight delay; they would come to the spa and spend the day with us. Many, so many of them, opened their hearts, sharing with us their life challenges, trusting and embracing the safety of the "stranger". They would always leave feeling lighter and more inspired from when they first arrived. It was for my staff and me an irreplaceable gratification. Flight attendants, passing through every week or every month, would make OraOxygen their focus point of their trip. We became their family they would visit on their way to Honk Kong, Beijing or Australia.

My vision for the company was to be located in all the major hub airports in the world. In order to do that I had to keep on answering "Request for Proposals", meeting with different airport authorities, and creating contacts and interests at various meetings and conferences. It was at one of those conferences in Phoenix, Arizona that I met Mr. Ed Kimmel, Manager of Business Development at Amsterdam Schiphol Airport. I felt this was another break for me. He listened to my ideas with an open mind, did not promise anything, but told me he would definitely get back to me. I felt encouraged by his true listening.

Simultaneously, using my Air Canada salary, I was able to hire someone to help me bring my vision to a higher level. I found the perfect executive assistant in Rosanna. At the time, a mother of one little boy; she was working from home and only ten minutes from our head office — my home. Rosanna became the dedicated, loyal and supportive assistant; adjusting her clock to my schedule — either I was in Toronto, Detroit, or Calgary. Later when it was time to expand our locations to Schiphol, Amsterdam, she would get up at 2:00 AM to be on the same time zone that I was. Thanks to her professional attitude, everyone thought that OraOxygen was run by a big corporate office. What a blast!

I certainly did not want to make the same mistake I had done before with the Center by not being at the spa in my first year. I went through many trials and errors to find a great manager for our Calgary location. A beautiful soul was sent to me with the name of Gregg, a gifted massage therapist who did not even know how big his gift was. He was definitely living his purpose in being a therapist. Instinctively knowing that I could trust him, I made him the manager. Perhaps not the wisest decision, as being a manager was not his calling. Nevertheless, in my staff I had found a wonderful team of people to help me accomplish the mission I had set for Ora. Each and every one of them had their own particular gift to give. Lots of magical hands, lots of compassion, and lots of loving souls. Sharing the same dream, and sharing the same vision, certainly makes a huge difference in a company's accomplishments. At last, I was living my life's purpose. "Making a positive difference in people's lives".

In 2002, it was time to open our second location. Another angel was sent to me with the name of Laura Baker. She was a hardworking Passenger Agent with Northwest Airlines who decided to leave the airline business, after eleven years, to join our team. Hired as a massage therapist, she almost instantly became our energetic charismatic manager for our Detroit location. I used to call her "my little ball of fire". She was full of love and energy and wonderful intentions, meanwhile having a clear view of the goals she would set for herself. During that time, Ed Kimmel had become a dear friend of mine, as well as several others at OraOxygen. He had come to visit us in Calgary and now in Detroit. Definitely this concept belonged in an international airport such as Schiphol. I was ready from my next goal…Amsterdam!

So there I was on a plane, on my way to meet with the designers and the airport authority. With the precious help of my dear friend, Annemarie, whom happens to be Dutch and living in Amsterdam, I was able to find a small apartment across the street from Amsterdam Central Station; an ideal location to travel to Amsterdam Schiphol. In four days I had to do a presentation to my investors, to show them where the company stood and what else needed to be done. I was ready and excited.

On the day of the big meeting I was confident that, after the presentation, we would finally take the company to the next level. *Passion, Purpose, Mission and Clarity* of the company's vision was all over me and in my PowerPoint presentation: Let's do it.

Let's give people what they want – and let's give me the resource support I need to professionally run my company. Let's bring this company to a successful *profitable* position that not only makes money but makes a huge difference in people's lives around the world including clients, employees, owners, travelers, etc…

The time had come! Wednesday, 1:00 PM. Meeting time.

***

What a shock when one hour later, not only were my very well researched requests denied, but I was asked to sign an agreement demoting me to the *manager* of the company. No rights in decision for growth, no resource support, I could be fired anytime, and at any executive's whim, with or without cause. I am sure some of you know what I am talking about; and if you don't, just know that I am sparing you all the ugly details.

For one full year, I did everything I could to buy my investors out and get the perfect "investor partner" by my side. With Stan's unconditional support and the help of our friend, Ed Kimmel, we did everything we could to find a suitable solution for everyone. What a draining experience it was. After months and months of fighting, and litigation lawyer negotiating, I found myself pressed to the wall. A wall that I did not know how to fight. A wall that was created out of greed and fear. How did they do that? How did that happen? How could they destroy someone's life so easily? Take away a person's life purpose on account of perceived profit margins and business perception? Why couldn't they see: they never invested in the spa business; they invested in me. In my *Passion*, my contagious *Enthusiasm*, my *Energy* and my *Vision*.

Pressed to the wall and paralyzed, I was living the worst day of my life as they callously left with my company, my dream, my child.

Imagine my surprise when what I thought was the worst day of my life, ended up to be the best.

Introduction to the Eleven Insights.

I never thought I would write a book. Especially not a book that would expose my vulnerability. But here you are with my book in your hands. You are about to discover the all-powerful insights that have changed my life. I did not invent them or create them. They were there all along below the surface of who I thought I was.

Each *in-sight* will teach you exactly what the word itself says — to see from *within*. And from *within* a door to new understanding and liberation will open before you: for the *Full Enjoyment of Your Life*.

I physically began writing this book in November 2010 but it's probably been here a long time before me, awaiting the moment to emerge. It is the result of living in fear for five painful years, and a lifetime of looking for answers to life.

In writing this book, I have healed the remainder of my emotional wounds. Many years ago a wonderful book called *A Course in Miracles* has taught me this:

Teach what you need to learn.

Today…My passion is to share what I love to learn.

CHAPTER FIVE

Insight 1 - Vulnerability

When we were children, we used to think that when we were grown-up we would no longer be vulnerable. But to grow up is to accept vulnerability...
To be alive is to be vulnerable.
Madeleine L'Engle
Author of Newbury Award Winner
A Wrinkle In Time

I start with vulnerability because vulnerability is at the base of all healing.

Healing from within must happen before any other healing can take place. After I lost my business, "my child", not only did I have to re-discover my passions, I had to uncover my vulnerability, and find my true self. Uncover my vulnerability? But I'd carefully kept it hidden all my life! I have never been afraid of stepping out of my comfort zone; I actually thrive on the opportunity of doing so; breaking down walls, as I have said before. But showing my vulnerability was taking me way further out of any comfort zone than I ever experienced before.

Surprisingly enough, in that moment at the seminar, standing in front of all those people with a microphone in my hands, even though my vulnerability was totally exposed, it felt like nothing could hurt me. I was not defensive, frightened, or embarrassed. I was just being in my totality, with my weaknesses, my tears, my honesty, my determination, and my sensitivity. Feeling my vulnerability for the first time! What a strange feeling. I squeezed the microphone tighter and kept on talking. This book is the result of my realization in that moment.

All of our lives we are led to believe that vulnerability is a weakness, something to hide, and something that does not feel good. That we need to protect ourselves, defend our dignity and way of life, anticipate the worst and live in scarcity; creating more separation, hostility and fear.

In order to embrace my vulnerability, this so called "weakness" of mine, I feel I need to start with what I know very well – my invulnerability.

My invulnerability, the one that keeps me

"protected", the one that keeps the distance between me and others, between my heart and other hearts.

Invulnerability, the one that does not allow any relationship to be complete; either a loving relationship, work relationship, or social relationship. There is always this wall of separation – no one really gets to know you for who you really are because your invulnerability is making sure of that. You never get to know anyone for who they really are because they do the same, and you mirror each other in your invulnerability.

Occasionally your invulnerability will let its wall down; and more often than not, it is with strangers. People who you will probably never see again in your life. How can they hurt you if you will never see them again? So it's okay to be who you truly are. When it comes to letting it go with the people closest to you, like your family, brothers and sisters, friends, coworkers, etc., then our invulnerability brings that wall back up like a river dam. They are too close, they will know you too much, they will discover the tools to hurt you, and there will be no more walls. So you decide to hide the beautiful spirit that you are, behind this big river dam of fear, where only a few drops of beauty are allowed to shine.

Then it becomes a vicious circle. Invulnerability attracts invulnerability. There, you are now surrounded with people as invulnerable as you are. An army of untouchable hearts on their way to glory. Please allow me to be sarcastic for a second or two, because that is what I believed all my life. I created this army for my "self". Which part of my self? Of course, the Ego. You got it. I will talk about this in another insight. One that will propel you into another way of being.

Having made myself invulnerable, I realize now it was out of fear. *You are only invulnerable when you are in fear.* What a thought! And yes a thought! It is all coming from the same place. Having been invulnerable all my life was something that my family could also always count on. In moments of drama, accidents, fights or disputes, death or sickness, one always needed to be in charge, in control. Who else than the invulnerable one? So how could I suddenly become vulnerable?

My first insight is about understanding Invulnerability before you can actually Embrace Your Vulnerability. Remember: Invulnerability attracts Invulnerability. Fear attracts Fear. So every time you find yourself in the space of wanting or pretending to be invulnerable, ask yourself these three questions:

1. What am I afraid of?
2. Which beautiful part of me is afraid to be seen?
3. Which sensitive part of me is afraid to be judged?

Only three questions; however they will always bring you back to the realization that your vulnerability is a gift. Take a moment now, to answer those three questions for yourself.

***

Before I share the true definition of this gift – vulnerability, let's look at some worldly definitions:

o Vulnerability is to be capable of being physically or emotionally wounded.

- Vulnerability is to be capable of being persuaded or tempted.
- And in a third meaning, the term "vulnerability" can also refer to a person who lets their guard down, leaving themselves open to censure or criticism.

However, the real meaning of vulnerability is much richer than these blurred definitions. Vulnerability is about choosing to be open to ourselves and to others. Looking back, I am not sure of which was the hardest one for me. I did feel that by letting others see my true sides; the good ones and the less good, the strong ones and the less strong, I was finally allowing it for myself. I have learned that none of my sides are bad or shameful. They just are what they are. They are part of the experience that makes each and every one of us the beautiful being that we are. Foremost, I have learned that having the ability to show our true sides at all times, invites others to do the same in a very comfortable and trusting manner. You realize that they are not much different than you.

How could I have not seen this before?

Soar With Vulnerability

Embracing our vulnerability is about being ourselves in our authenticity, in total trust; in the realization that there is nothing or anyone to fear. Being ourselves requires us to let go of the façade that we think we are.

Because of this façade or personality that we have created for ourselves, as a defense mechanism, we have become the actor of our illusionary life, creating false beliefs, stories, and disconnections. Vulnerability is not about stories.

Vulnerability is about letting go of the "endless reality" of our stories.

Let me explain. Your stories are products of your mind. And your mind always lives in the past or the future; never in the present. Only the present is real therefore endless. It just is. It doesn't have a beginning nor does it have an end. And because we believe our stories, we make our reality endless. There is only one reality, only one truth.

Just imagine being in the presence of an amazing sunset. This is reality. Can you allow yourself to be with the splendor of its colors? Be overwhelmed by its beauty?

Just be with what the reality is? Can you be

without words, without mind, without thought?

From the moment you start describing the sunset, and saying how beautiful it is, you have left reality and moved into your stories, your mind.

In my five year quest to regain my passion, I travelled to Tanzania, Africa and I felt a glimpse of that "reality". The beauty of the reality I felt "in the moment" was completely overwhelming, awe-inspiring, and breathtaking; all I could do was cry. These tears were not of sadness. These were tears of gratefulness for the endless reality of life. I let myself be part of the reality, receiving the love, the inspiration and the energy. Or may I say "Innergy", as it is truly an inside experience. One that requires our full attention.

When you embrace your vulnerability, you are starting to let go of your stories, of old beliefs, of your false protection, your illusionary self; there are no more pretenses, no more guards, and no more deception. Vulnerability is unguarded and Truth can finally resurface. The ultimate truth, the one that sits comfortably in the unknown.

It's the truth that never needs to be questioned, only experienced. You will feel freer than ever before, with no thoughts cluttering your mind, no judgments about what should and what shouldn't be.

Vulnerability could be spelled the same way as Respons-Ability. It means that it is your ability to respond to, as it is your ability to be vulnerable. It is your ability to live the true you. Using this ability, the truth shows you that being vulnerable means to be ready to live in insecurity.

Not the "social insecurity" as one would think, but as in the "insecurity of the unknown". I will talk about this further in the book, so be sure to keep on reading and you will learn this other important secret.

To be vulnerable is not about being weak, fragile or powerless; even though society would like you to think so. Vulnerability is about having the desire to be honest, and having openness with yourself and others. Vulnerability is expressing yourself, as to what and who you are, with focus and clarity. Vulnerability is part of the experience that makes you the beautiful being that you are. Vulnerability is your strength, your untainted power.

Each and every one of us is dealing with the fear of being vulnerable, until we realize that vulnerable is all this and more. Vulnerability or invulnerability is the result of your own thoughts. I will explain this in the last three insights.

I realize that by embracing my vulnerability I am ready to let go and prepared to accept my life in its entirety. I feel open and receiving. I am definitely ready for all of that. Now I can finally be free.

Or so I thought! One more step was required. I had to **Surrender**.

CHAPTER SIX

Insight 2 - Surrender

The measure of a man or woman's power can be found in the depth of their surrender.
William Booth
Founder of the Salvation Army

I had to surrender. Surrender to my *self*, my true emptiness.

What is true emptiness? It is not about creating isolation. It is about diving into the infinite source of life where all truth is, and all answers are. In emptiness lays our fullness. In order to feel this fullness, one needs to surrender. I had to surrender.

I was never one to surrender. For me to surrender meant to give up, to quit. Giving up and quitting would have implied a weakness on my part, a lack of courage, a demonstration of vulnerability. Because previously I had made myself invulnerable, I just could not surrender.

Just like vulnerability, the meaning of the word surrender has been misunderstood, and is still misinterpreted by many of us. Surrender comes along with some type of negative intonations such as not being strong enough, or courageous enough. Some would go as far to say that when you surrender you are being a coward.

Once again, and unfortunately, this is what we are led to believe in our modern society. When we surrender, we give our power to someone else, making them stronger than we are. This way of thinking is induced inside our mind at a very young age, and we carry it with us in everything that we do.

Part of my growing and healing experiences took me to Bodhgaya, India for a spiritual retreat with Andrew Cohen, Spiritual teacher and Founder of EnlightenNext. We would meditate three times a day, and each meditation would be followed with teachings from Andrew. In the first week we were guided into the "letting go". At the end of the week, Andrew shared his surprise at realizing how many of us had no understanding of what it means to let go. We were having difficulty letting go of our physical distraction while in meditation. Not letting go of our physical discomfort, itchiness, coldness, tiredness. Not letting go of our thoughts. Therefore, not surrendering.

That night after a deeper and longer meditation, it all came to me as I was walking back to my sleeping quarters. Surrendering is about having the willingness to let everything be as it is. And as you surrender there is a beautiful calmness that penetrates you, and you just know that you are not in charge anymore. Creation is.

Life is. Whatever is, is. Whatever will be, will be. Sounds like defeatism? There is no defeat, no win or lose. There is only acceptance of what is, of reality. The true reality.

Here I was, standing in the darkness of India, admiring the surrendering of nature. Looking up at the sky with its shining stars, I let myself once again be part of the magic of the only true reality, watching life around me in the moment.

The tree is being the tree, the wind is being the wind, the rain is being the rain. When did you ever see a tree trying to be the wind? Never.

The tree is letting the wind be the wind,

bending under its embrace, surrendering to its caresses and its immense hug. The tree is letting be and letting go. Total surrendering of being what it is in its entirety, and letting the other be what it is in its totality. There is no judgment only harmony.

In Tanzania, Africa I surrendered to the beauty and harmony of endless living creatures. The crane standing on the back of the hippopotamus, the Pink Flamingos drinking out of the same water as the zebras and the wildebeest, and small tiny birds hitching a ride on the back of an elephant or a hippo.

Everything was just perfect the way it was. None of the animals were trying to be or do something that was not of their purpose in life. The zebra was not trying to fly, and the bird was not trying to roll in the mud. They were just being who they are. Only we, human beings, want to be something else than what and who we are. Once again I was reminded of the freedom of surrendering.

It took a lot of work and inquiries: an enlightening trip to India, an inspiring trip to Africa, lots of money spent on numerous seminars, many self-help books, a lot of pain — and mostly a microphone, to finally be able to surrender.

Soar With Vulnerability

In the willingness of surrendering, everything becomes much simpler and more natural. In surrendering there is no more need for resistance, defense, or opinion. No more opinion of what is or what is not. Everything is what is, because it is.

What a realization!

Once you let go of the thoughts of what that something should be, you finally allow for that something to be what it is. With no involvement whatsoever except for the one of observer. Surrendering is about surrendering to ourselves. It is about being our true selves, whatever it is that we are, and accepting total responsibility for it. Let our soul be! Just **Let it Be**. The Beatles certainly felt surrender when they wrote:

And when the broken hearted people
Living in the world agree,
There will be an answer, let it be.
For though they may be parted there is
Still a chance that they will see
There will be an answer, let it be.
Let it be, let it be. Yeah,
There will be an answer, let it be.

In my surrendering, I allowed forgiveness to take place; forgiveness of my investor's judgments, of my painful experience, and mostly of myself. Forgiveness of all my fears and my judgments about them.

True forgiveness is about being grateful for that experience, and expressing thankfulness for the opportunity to expand. In forgiveness there is no more darkness, no more grief, and no more confusion.

Surrender and be on the way to YOU! You in your ultimate "I" is present to listen and to receive the kindness and the love that you are.

Sur-render is to give honor to all that is. Even if all there is, is **Pain.**

CHAPTER SEVEN

Insight 3 - Pain

That which is your perception, is but a creation of your mind. Your thoughts are nothing more than reactions to what you perceive you have experienced in the past.
Journey Beyond Words, Brent Haskell.

I did not realize that by becoming invulnerable I had created a world of bigger pain for myself. The pain of not allowing myself to feel "true pain". True pain is not there to hurt us or punish us. On the contrary, true pain is a "divine sign". A sign to help us recognize that we have been ignoring something or blocking someone from our life, usually our own selves. True pain is an opportunity for expansion.

Pain can be mental, physical, or emotional. Pain is a sensation that usually is associated with *hurt*. In Louise Hay's book, *Heal Your Body*, it is said that the probable cause of any pain is *guilt*. And guilt always seeks punishment. Wow! Therefore your punishment is to be in pain.

If this is true, how can we listen to our pain, let go of it, and let go of the guilt as well? How do we find out where the pain that we are experiencing is really coming from? If the probable cause of pain is guilt, the source of the pain must be from the past, as guilt doesn't exist in the now.

The other night I went to bed very early because I was in pain — in physical pain. In the previous days, I had been getting severe stomach and abdominal pain; sudden and intense pain. I fell asleep on my stomach pushing my belly into a pillow.

I woke up at 3:00 AM with the pain acting up again. So instead of fighting the pain, I started to listen to the message.

As I stopped to listen to the message I decided to embrace the pain along with the *no-pain* and feel the silence in between.

Pain is not of the soul, pain is not of the spirit. Pain is of the physical which includes the emotional and the mental. We don't consciously ask for pain, unless we are a masochist. So if pain is given to us, there must be a reason for it. Maybe even a lesson?

Pain is a signal that your higher consciousness is trying to communicate something to you. Something important enough that only the pain can stop you; only pain can force you to take the time to listen. Sometimes the message can be as simple as "make more time for yourself" or just to "slow down".

Up until recently we used to live, or choose to believe that we live, in a world of opposites. Hot and cold, sun and rain, light and dark, love and fear. We no longer live in a world of duality, but in a world of Oneness. Therefore, *pain* is an opportunity to appreciate the *no-pain*. The state of well-being and the blessings that come with it. It is a lesson in never taking anything for granted. Pain is a contribution for our appreciation. An appreciation for all that we have, including the pain. Sharing your pain is also a gift, just like sharing your vulnerability.

Let me explain. Pain is a gift when we choose to accept that it is there for a particular teaching for ourselves or others. *It is in the sharing of our learning or lessons from the pain that it becomes that gift.*

When we find ourselves in a situation that becomes a pain (problem), we usually only focus on the problem, and we lose sight of the benefit of this particular situation. Once again, if the probable cause of pain is guilt, as mentioned in Louise Hay's book *Heal Your Body*, then the source of the pain must be from the past, as guilt doesn't exist in the NOW.

Whether a life situation is great or not, it all depends on the way our mind perceives and interprets it. What we experience physically in our humanness is always a perception, a creation of our mind. What we see with our physical eyes is also perception. What we see and what we perceive is just that…perception.

The reality of who we are lies behind that world we see. Therefore, the real essence of who we are does not experience the illusional pain.

What about emotional and mental pain? Where is it coming from? Are we creating it ourselves through our thoughts, our belief system, and our concepts of what is right or wrong? Is there a right or wrong? And if so, what makes it so, who decides?

Let's say something happens like "I lost my company." And I did *lose* my company. Why does it hurt? When does it start hurting? What kind of pain is it?

If everything comes from within and not from the outside that means pain would be self-inflicted. So have I inflicted this pain upon myself? Have I inflicted the pain, or have I inflicted thoughts upon me, about my loss? Thoughts are never impartial. Our thoughts are always and nothing more than reactions. Reactions to past perceptions.

The hurt starts when we look at the experience from the *loss* and *defeat* point of view and not the *win* and *expand* point of view. We perceive that we have lost something; often before we even own it. Therefore our thoughts react to the perceived loss and we start believing those thoughts.

Let me explain. I had lost my business; that was a fact. Where was the win? I could not see it. I could not see the possibility that there could be a gain in there for me. It took me a while to notice and recognize that this visible loss was there to force me to create something different...something that would have a different impact on my *expansion*. Like writing this book perhaps.

There is never any real loss, as in every perceived loss we uncover the true gift. But why is it hurting? Is it the thoughts that I have about losing my company? Or is it the story that I make with the thoughts about losing my company?

I perceived that I had lost something. My soul's purpose. My thoughts reacted to the perceived loss and I started believing these thoughts.

Pain is just what your thoughts make about what you perceive. Why does it hurt? Because thoughts have to make some things right and some things wrong. Knowing that perception is just a perception, it is not real, by changing our thoughts we will change our perceived reality. What we believe creates *our* reality as well as our limitations. It is a never ending circle because then it goes right to our "emotional system".

I realized at that moment that I had the choice. I could choose painful thoughts or peaceful thoughts. When I had my company, I was always too busy to socialize, to visit my friends or my family. My life had become focused on work and on growing the company. I was working seven days a week, twelve to fifteen hours per day. And even when I was not actually working, all I could think about or talk about was OraOxygen. It had become my life. I had vanished into it.

After losing my company, I said to myself one day: "What if I could erase all thoughts of my memory? By erasing the thoughts, the beliefs would go away along with my emotional pain." Could that actually work? Every time we think an old thought, we also awake with it whatever pain was related to it. Could I choose only peaceful thoughts? Could I remove the thought hence the pain that came with it?

Try it. Just for a moment be with one thought that brings you pain. A thought of unfairness, envy, or guilt. A thought of what you perceive that other people have done to you. Or of events that happened which initiated resentment, depression, judgment, or anger.

What if you could erase all these thoughts and replace them with thoughts that bring you peace, joy, and clarity? Take one thought at a time and be with it.

See how you could modify it so it brings you happiness instead of pain. Do the same thing with your belief. How does your belief become your truth?

***

I did not stop there. It was time to break another wall — create a new language.

As everything is energy, I felt I needed to eliminate some words out of my vocabulary. Words such as: *should, but, can't, doubt,* and replaced them with *could, and, can* and *trust*. I did the same with any other words that tend to judge or condemn myself or someone else.

Any words of judgment or condemnation bring pain. When we are in pain, we are in fear. When we are in fear, we know that our ego is there somewhere, playing tricks on us. And that's the challenging part.

How can you recognize that your pain is really coming from fear? How can you accept that your pain is created by your own ego? How do you look

Soar With Vulnerability

"within"? How do you look "inside" of you? How do you alleviate the pain?

You need to stop and listen — once you have stopped, embrace and accept all thoughts without judging them. Just be aware of your beliefs about them. Now, you can choose to keep these thoughts or not. You can choose to keep the thoughts and just change all beliefs about them. You can choose to create new possibilities for each one of them.

Then let it go. This might sound easier to say than to do. Your thoughts need to blame something or someone, defend and justify. Just let them go. You are now free to be the conscious creator that you were always meant to be.

When pain enters your life, whether it's mental, emotional, or physical pain, you want to welcome it as much as you would welcome a dozen white roses, or as one of the best gifts you have ever received.

I am not talking about the pain that someone has when hit by a truck or when aggressively beaten or experiencing a third degree burn. I am talking about welcoming the pain that comes after the initial pain. Let me explain: If you experience a third degree burn on your body, of course it hurts and is very painful. After proper medical care, the pain will gradually go away. You are now left with the second pain. The one you will have to deal with for the rest of your life — the scars. Stop resisting. They are part of you as you are part of them.

I know it sounds extreme and perhaps even crazy right now, but from the moment you stop resisting the pain, you allow a space for this new creative energy to find its way to communicate with you. *Everything is energy*. It is what you do with this new energy that will dictate the new outcome of this experience. There is a famous quote about these choices we all have and it goes like this: *It's not what happens to you, but how you react to it that matters.*

Take for instance the example of Nick Vujicic. Born without legs and arms, he felt empty and helpless. Growing up, he was looked upon as a freak by many. Did he wallow in self-pity and defeatism? No he did not. Today, Nick travels the world as a motivational speaker, writes books, and is an inspiration to all. Nick believes that there is a purpose in each of the struggles we all encounter in our lives, and that our attitude toward those struggles can be the keys to overcoming the challenges we face.

It is exactly the same thing with pain.

When you look back on your life and remember all the different types of pain you have experienced, ask yourself, "What would have happened if I had acted on its first warning sign, instead of resisting it?"

- o *Would you have stayed in that relationship for as long as you did?*
- o *Would you have had to go through this triple bypass surgery?*
- o *Would you have had to undertake major self-esteem therapy?*

When you don't choose for yourself, when you don't decide what the best is for you and don't take "response-ability" for all of your thoughts, decisions, and feelings you are living *unconsciously*.

Have I been *unconsciously unconscious* all of my life? Have you?

It is time to listen and live your **Authenticity.**

CHAPTER EIGHT

Insight 4 -Authenticity

It is an insult to your Self to be born, live, and die without knowing the answer to the mystery of why you were sent here as a human being in the first place.
Paramahansa Yogananda

What a wonderful quote. I would like to follow it with this other profound one by William Barclay: *There are two great days in a person's life — the day we are born and the day we discover why.*

Why am I here? What is my *why*?

I found myself with no role to play, not even the invulnerable one. I had no performance to perform, and I did not have any anticipation or expectation. I found myself in the moment — in the awareness of each moment. I embraced the acceptance of it all.

Once you embrace your vulnerability and surrender to all there is, even pain, you are left with *you* in its purest form — your *authenticity*. What is authenticity? What does it mean to be authentic? How will you know when you are truly authentic? Have you ever asked yourself questions such as: Who am I? What am I supposed to do? What is my mission? What is my purpose?

I ask myself these questions often. Sometimes I know the answers, it is crystal clear, and other times it is all blurry. And it keeps on going: Am I living the life I am supposed to live? Am I honest with myself and others? Am I doing things just to please others? Am I doing these things because people expect them from me?

***

When was the last time you stopped and asked yourself some of these questions? Do you feel complete, fulfilled and in harmony with yourself? If you are reading this book it might be because you are asking yourself these questions right now. If you are, pay close attention.

From the moment you experience your authenticity, your true self, you will not want to be anything else but *authentic*.

Soar With Vulnerability

When you are authentic you know it right away because you feel good, real good. You are in perfect alignment with who you really are, and everything flows.

At times, your authenticity will perturb some people. This disturbance does not belong to you but to them. Inauthenticity wants inauthenticity. Or as the saying goes, "Misery loves company." Remain in the truth of your true nature and witness wonders happening—including the other authentic people you attract into your life.

Starting many thousands of years ago, we all have been sent here on planet Earth to live our *human* experience, to fulfill our mission. Many of us have forgotten the reality of our true nature, our origin. We have come to believe that we are *human beings*. And if we are not human beings what are we?

Scientists, theologians, researchers, etc., will come up with a variety of different answers. We are energy, we are part of the star system, etc. Disputing our origin or what we really are, is not the purpose of my book. Therefore, I will simply say that my own view on the human being subject is that, it is a wonderful creation of the universe. As part of this creation, I believe I am here to live this experience in order to expand and perhaps, return to the common source.

Being here as a human being is a wonderful gift, and I choose to be totally involved. As I do, I notice that my being is constantly evolving, expanding with every new experience. To be totally involved, you need to be authentic. In order to be authentic, you have to know who you are. *Once you have the cellular understanding that you are limitless, you will engage fully and live your life truthfully.* Once you know who you are, you own your life; you show up truly and completely.

What you think about what you think you are is another form of limitation and constraint.

I strongly suggest you read this phrase a couple of times, and let it sink into your being. Let's take a moment to do so.

What you think about what you think you are is another form of limitation and constraint.

Soar With Vulnerability

For instance, when I believed I was a failure I thought nobody would respect me for my creative entrepreneurship ever again, nor would they look up to me for other projects, or they'd just plainly not want to be with me. My thinking about who I believed I was, was purely a judgment; therefore it was limiting my boundless being.

Instead of ruminating about who you think you are or might be, start feeling and listening more to the vibrations coming from within you. Identify who's actually there under all those layers of thoughts, and why it is all perfect as it is.

Everything you think about yourself is reflected in everything you do in life; consciously or unconsciously. The next insight will explain the importance of living consciously. So please make sure you keep on reading.

In the meantime:

- *If a doctor needed to remove your right arm, are you still you? Yes.*
- *If he had to remove your left leg, are you still you? Yes.*

- *If she performed a liver transplant on you, are you still you? Yes.*

So who are you? What is you?

Take a moment to find your center. The place where there are no thoughts. There is no breathing, no mind, no emotions, no body, and still you are. Can you feel it? Can you feel that who you are is much more, and much bigger than your body?

Some of us see ourselves as human beings having a spiritual experience. Others prefer to say that they are *spiritual beings having a human experience*. Who knows? But once you have the true understanding, this is when you truly get the gift of life you have been given.

All "I" know is that either as a human being or as a spiritual being, I am here on earth with a mission to accomplish. You are too.

How do I know that? I just know. It comes from a higher place of knowing. After losing my company, I thought *I had lost it*. Familiar with that expression? Had I gone crazy? No, I had lost my spirituality and that special place of knowing. Today, I know it was just another thought I had chosen to believe.

Soar With Vulnerability

We all have that special place of knowingness. The place where there are no doubts, no hesitation, no wonders. Each one of us has a different mission to fulfill, a different gift to give, a unique calling to answer. I decided on *reality;* now, in this world, on this planet, in this physical body, in my temporary suit. I elect to believe that I am a *spirit in reality*. In reality with all there is, now.

I realized that by being who I am openly in my authenticity I also get to know others truly. By living your authentic uniqueness, you are fulfilling your divine mission. And don't be surprised to find out that your purpose fits you to perfection.

Here are some examples of people who have lived their uniqueness and the great things they have accomplished in doing so. Let's start with Albert Einstein, father of modern physics, Martin Luther King, symbolic leader of American blacks and world figure, John Lennon, lover of peace and social causes, Gandhi, father of a nation, and Mother Teresa, founder of the Missionaries of Charity, award winner of multiple Noble Prizes.

Other examples closer to your heart could be Oprah, philanthropist, television pioneer, producer, etc., Richard Branson, Knight of Entrepreneurship, or even Lady Gaga, who is making flamboyant contributions to the music industry.

What is your unique contribution?

I finally embrace my *uniqueness.* In my uniqueness resides my greatness. There is no need to look for it anymore. It is "I". It's been "I" all along. The same applies to you. Your uniqueness rises in its transparency, lightness, and happiness. Your greatness, your mission will find you as it is YOU. So once again, just surrender and listen to the signals from within YOU.

Knowing myself from a higher self place, and living my authenticity, is one of the most challenging and exciting opportunities I have created in my life. Some of us probably won't take that opportunity in this lifetime, and this is indeed unfortunate.

Successful people move on their own initiative,
and they know where they are going before they start
Napoleon Hill

Soar With Vulnerability

In the book, *What You Think of Me Is None of My Business*, Dr. Whittaker talks about the four truths. The fourth being: "You have made decisions about yourself, others, and life that was once conscious decisions, but have become unconscious ones and yet continue to direct your decisions and to determine the quality of your life."

Powerful stuff wouldn't you say? Is your life's blueprint made out of your beliefs, which are mostly a recollection and misinterpretation of your very early life experiences, even previous lives? Or is the outline already designed and conducted from an invisible strand, connecting you to a higher source?

The truth is that it's all entangled as one and causing misinterpretations for each of us. We all use these misconceptions on each other *unconsciously* and a lot of the time *consciously*. We get so caught up in pleasing others, or reacting to their *misinterpretation* of us, that we don't realize our life is not about us, it is about *them.* Let me give you a simple example: You love to dance. Your partner does not. Nevertheless, Friday night comes and you go dancing with your friends. Your partner stays at home and watches his favorite movies on DVDs. And the two of you are completely comfortable with this arrangement. The first misinterpretation comes from a woman who thinks she cannot do the same as you. After all, it would not be appropriate, being a married woman and all. Therefore she judges you from her own boundaries, and lays a heavy guilt trip on you.

People see us through their own comfort or discomfort zone and judge us for being who we are. We keep on correcting or adjusting who we are to please their misinterpretation, and to *fit in*. Just to fit in with them. They do precisely the same with others.

How do you recognize when you are playing that game?

***

First, you've got to STOP — really stop and become the witness. Become the observer of your own life. Notice your thoughts, your busyness, and your shallowness.

Become aware of your body reactions. Are you open? Are you closed? Are you anxious? Or are you peaceful? How does it feel to be you?

Soar With Vulnerability

Now, become aware of the people around you. The ones who push your buttons the most, and the ones who never do. Notice the difference in your reactions around different people. Who do you enjoy being with? Who are you having difficulty loving? You might feel some negativity toward some people, or even some apprehension, don't judge it. Just keep on observing. Observing as if you are not involved.

Through this simple exercise you will realize that most of your life you have made decisions that were not based on your authenticity — rather on misinterpretations of others, and your own; unconscious decisions that might appear conscious, but that were planted when you were an infant or a small child. These seeds sit in your *subconscious mind* until a particular trigger wakes them up. Authenticity is about *You Being You*.

The rain is being the rain, the tree is being the tree, and the rock is being the rock.

You Be You.

Your divine origin [inspiration] has given you a mission to accomplish and that is the meaning

Suzanne Letourneau

*[purpose] of your life here.
Use your natural talents [strength], your desire to make and create [action] a positive memorable difference in this world.*

Once you have clearly understood the power of *authenticity* you are unstoppable. I now live my authenticity. I am alive and real. I make "conscious decisions". Decisions that are not based on misinterpretations or make believe.

I would like to invite you to do the same.

And once again the work doesn't stop here. You may think that being authentic is something that comes naturally. Unfortunately, it doesn't always do so. One also needs to learn and practice **Conscious Awareness**.

CHAPTER NINE

Insight 5 - Conscious Awareness

*You are the consciousness and awareness
beyond words and thoughts.
Being fully conscious, yet without thoughts,
is like sleep, but yet being awake.*
Remez Sasson

Is awareness an ability, a learned skill, or a natural state of being? For me the meaning of the word *awareness* has become so simple and yet so profound.

Aware- [being] **ness**
It is the knowing-ness of your being-ness
And in your being-ness you know that you are beyond
Anything you think yourself to be.
To be more precise **be-in**[g]-**ness**
Is your natural state of be-ing versus be-coming.
It is inward not outward.
It is in your power.

Conscious Awareness is the willingness to be awake. It is the decision to be present in each and every moment. To live in conscious awareness requires you to be the action, and the witness of the action at all times, *all the time*. The more risk, the more insecurity, the more you will be drawn to live your life in "conscious awareness". And living your life in conscious awareness brings this new possibility of the more powerful *security of the unknown* versus the weaker *security of the known*. I will discuss this in more depth in Chapter Fourteen, Insight #10. So be sure to stay tuned to receive this powerful insight.

For now, just imagine having someone standing behind you, supervising each and every move you do, all the time. You are doing the action, and that someone behind {you} watching you, is also you, observing {you} the action.

We are the actors and the directors of our own movie. Each one of us is also one of the many actors in the movie we call "Life". The part that we play has nothing to do with who we genuinely are. When the movie comes to "The End", we will get up and return to who we truly are.

Soar With Vulnerability

Together let's stop and carefully observe and examine our lives as it is right here and now. Choose to be *consciously conscious*.

1. What are you aware of? Are you aware of when you follow your mind? Do you know when you follow your heart? Or do you even question that? Are you simply on "automatic pilot"?
2. What is the source of your happiness now? Does it come from a relationship? Or perhaps, from pursuing a successful career? Does it come from outside your self or from within?
3. Does your awareness force you to reexamine your life? Do you ever stop to introspect?
4. Are you aware of your thoughts? Are you attentive to where your thoughts are coming from? Do you question them, or just let them dictate to you?
5. Are you the *observed* or the *observer* of your life?

How many of these questions can you answer honestly and without any doubts? Do you ever feel desperate for answers, and everywhere you look, there is nothing? What do you do when you recognize that there is nothing left inside of you?

When I was faced with the fact that there was nothing left inside of me, I chose to be *consciously aware*. I chose to be honest about it. That honesty taught me that simply by acknowledging it, I had made my first step toward the inner freedom of consciousness. All that time I had not realized that I had become *unconsciously unconscious* of my gifts, my blessings, and my unique calling.

What does it mean to be *unconsciously unconscious*? In a very simple way, to be unconscious is to live your life out of the moment, out of the now, right now. And to be unconsciously unconscious means that you don't even know that you are doing it. The unconscious mind is the state of mind we create when we decide not to live in "conscious awareness" at all times, in every moment.

When you decide to live your life in conscious awareness versus unconsciously unconscious, your whole life transforms. It opens up to a whole new

Soar With Vulnerability

world of possibilities. There is no more limitation. You are now facing the wonderful world of creation. You are the true creator of your thoughts, of your life in authenticity.

***

Have you ever heard the expression: "Seize the day before the day seizes you"?

It is the same thing with your entire life. It's all about embracing your life and every moment in it, and of it. Every time you experience joyfulness or happiness, know that you have created it. This is what you have chosen for yourself at that moment. Every time you experience sadness, or anger, know that you have chosen it for yourself at that very same moment.

What do you mean I have chosen it for myself? I chose to create sadness or anger in my life? That's preposterous!

You have chosen to create that experience for yourself right now, in your authenticity. Your subconscious mind is presenting you with what you have created for yourself in order to remind you of who you are.

Your subconscious mind is like a computer

where you have stored different software. It runs automatically in the background allowing the conscious mind to deal with chosen actions in the now. Your conscious mind delegates responsibilities to the subconscious mind. Once that assignment is completed, the subconscious mind sends responses to the conscious mind in the form of emotions.

Let me explain. Your subconscious mind feeds on whatever you send it. It is a little bit like a jelly fish in the ocean. It floats around with no real sense of direction until a *thought* surfaces. Your subconscious mind reacts automatically to your thought, and automatically sends you an emotional message for you to respond to. It all happens instantly.

When you decide to be the true creator, you choose to be in harmony with your subconscious and conscious mind. You embrace full responsibility and whole involvement. You live your truth and you are conscious of it.

Once I made that recognition, I decided to be *consciously conscious* as the *creator that I am*. In the next few insights you will learn the power of clarity, passion, freedom and emptiness. Take a moment to erase all knowledge you think you have, all goals you might have, and step into YOU. You are in for a great adventure.

Are you ready for it? Your new adventure starts with **Clarity.**

CHAPTER TEN

Insight 6 - Clarity

*"When you act accordingly to your principles you are being dishonest because when you act according to **what you think you ought to be**, you are **not** what you are"*
Jiddu Krishnamurti

You have now been given the first five insights. How do you feel? Are you starting to feel lighter? Are you starting to feel like you never really allowed yourself to be YOU? Maybe you are a little confused, or even at loss on what to do next.

So what is the next step?

It is about being clear. It is finding Clarity.

Clarity is about knowing and living your life essentials. Your life essentials are your passions. Your passions come to you every day under many different forms and signs. They come to you as *whispers*. Whispers so soft that often you don't even hear them. Do the whispers come and go as they please? Or is it just that sometimes you choose to hear them, and sometimes not? Sometimes you just have a sense of them, and already they are out of reach.

Each and every one of us has a unique calling, a sole [soul] purpose. This is what your passions are trying to tell you. So you need to pay attention.

You need to be present to receive the soft messages. Stand still, be quiet. Start to *listen* and *see*, with your true eyes and ears – the true essence that you are.

Clarity of mind means clarity of passion;
this is why a great and clear mind
loves ardently and sees distinctly what he loves
Blaise Pascal

To find your passions, **you also have to dare to want to be even more of who you think you are.** You have to be honest with yourself throughout your whole being. Let's read that phrase once again and be with it: **You also have to dare to want to be even more of who you think you are.**

Soar With Vulnerability

How do you do that?

You want to connect consciously with your *unconditioned self*, the core of who you are. Your heart is the entrance to your unconditioned self.

Let's step back for a moment. If you know and accept that everything comes from within you, and all that is outside of you is not actually real, then where would you presume your *unconditioned self* to be?

The unconditioned self is the part of you that is not affected by the outside. It is the one that is not disturbed by the unconscious mind or the subconscious mind. It is **pure self** without conditions. Pure self is Love. Consequently, if **pure self is love**, the "unconditioned self" is truly "unconditional love", isn't it? Not that complicated when we look at it that way.

Now that you know that, let's go into your unconditioned self, your unconditional love; the source of you, the source of all. How does it feel? Is there any noise in there? How about chaos or confusion? How about fear and doubt? Are you alone? Let's take a look at it together. Let me transport you to a place of unconditional love.

First, I entered the water with the noise of my brain, my doubts, and my confusion. I am alone in the wilderness of the ocean. I am alone swimming. Swimming with the wild Dolphins. Alone, I AM, being with Oneness. All-one with the Source. I have my first close encounter.

It is magic! Pure love is all over and around me. My new friend is looking at me with his beautiful smile, and I find myself looking back into his deep profound eyes. In this moment, time as we know it, does not exist anymore. There is just that moment in the moment. It is him and I, in truth, *in love*. Nothing else matters as there is nothing else but love. And at that moment we are it — Pure Love. Our *unconditioned self*!

Clarity comes from this place of pure love. Clarity is when you just *know*. And that knowing is much bigger than all that you *think you know*. There are no questions, no doubts, no investigation. Only simplicity and transparency.

Clarity is when you don't need to question anymore. If you need to question, it is because you have moved from your place of true higher knowingness into your lower knowing. The one that is restricting you, the one that is judging you.

True knowing is about living YOU.

The only questions you want to ask your higher knowingness on a regular basis might be: "**Am I fulfilling my mission with the gifts I have been offered? Am I living my truth in authenticity?**" Allow your feelings, positive or negative, to reflect the answer. Take a moment now to ask yourself these questions. Be with the questions. Feel the answer coming to your heart.

What has been given to you is unique to you. Have you recognized it yet?

- What is your gift?
- Are you sharing this gift? Or are you purely neglecting it?
- What is it that you love to do most?
- What have you always been attracted to, since you've been a little boy, a little girl?
- What keeps on coming back as a source of fulfillment in your life?

Start looking at the signs. These signs will guide

you directly to your passions; consequently your distinctive mission, your purpose will show itself.

What about clarity? Why is it so important to have clarity in our hearts, in our lives? *Once you have **clarified what you value most**, and you have identified what those things would actually look like in the real world, then and only then, will you have the inner-motivation to increase your personal power, improve your performance and take responsibility for making those things come true for you.* (from the book *Success on Purpose* by E.R. Haas & Kent C. Madson.)

Clarity is pure energy. Once you are clear about your mission, your whole outlook on life is transformed. Your *shoulds* become your *musts*, your *coulds* become your *dos*, and your *doubts* become your *truths*.

Once you know without a doubt what your **why** is, your **what** and your **how** will follow. Defining the why and understanding the why is key to living your purpose. Steve Jobs, Founder of Apple, was running his company from HIS WHY! *The WHY does not come from looking ahead at what you want to achieve. The WHY comes by examining those times when everything just "felt right" and you loved* *the experience – when you were living your WHY – you will uncover the keys to discovering and articulating your personal WHY.* Simon Sinek

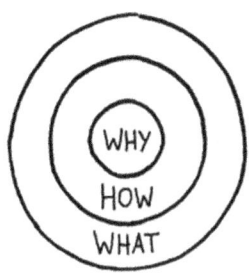

Your **_why_** is the fuel that gives you the determination. In integrity, your **_why_** creates the persistence needed to do whatever it takes to pursue your dreams.

The *why* is your purpose and the driving force in time of challenge or difficulties, to keep you on track. Your *why* is your heart center.

In *A Year of Growing Rich* (Napoleon Hill), he says: *Once we understand the broad purpose of life, we become reconciled to the circumstances that force us to struggle. As a result, we accept struggle for what it is –*

opportunity. He continues, *By running to embrace struggle, rather than trying to avoid it, you, too, can use it to help you learn, grow and succeed.*

The struggles, the difficulties, are solely opportunities to challenge you in knowing yourself and life more. Opportunities to free yourself through making choices for change.

Who you are at *essence* attracts the situations you need. Each situation has a reason. As you are reading this, you might think that I am not making sense. But if you take a moment to be with everything that has happened in your life, you will easily realize that each and every single one of them have made you the wonderful person you are today. It is not about being the strongest; it is not about being the best, or being the one that people expect you to be. It is about the recognition of your experiences; experience per experience.

What do you need to understand from that situation? Perhaps it is something that you need to let go of, or simply something to *open up to* for change?

The understanding of our complex simplicity doesn't come all at once for the *unconscious*

unconscious. It is a practice, a progression. It is a de-cluttering. A spring cleaning of all that we think we know, and of all that we think we don't know.

As human beings we *think* we know. As soul beings we just know.

Inspiration is the work of your Divine. Divine has given you your passions. Have you discovered yours yet? Or have you buried it and lost the key?

In the next insight I will share my secret to rekindling my passions. I invite you to join me, and give yourself this gift of reviving your **Passion.**

CHAPTER ELEVEN

Insight 7 - Passion

Passion is Power.

I have no special talents, I am only passionately curious
Albert Einstein.

Based on the fundamental meaning of each letter I have created my own definition of the word *passion:*

Purpose: The meaning, the mission of my life
Action: What I do to make a difference, what is meaningful
Sincerity: Being authentic and transparent to myself and others
Strength: Sharing my talents, my gifts
Inspiration: Living a true connection with the heart
Opportunity: Limitless, the choice of being free
Natural: Peace, inner silence.

In order to find yourself you will need to find your *heart's passions*. They will make you come alive naturally, no questions asked. It is there for you to enjoy!

Here's my secret:

*Passion is about choosing to be free, by being authentic and transparent
to yourself and others.*

*Passion is about making a legendary difference in people's lives
by sharing your unique gifts.*

Passion is about living in peace with your vulnerability, and by making a true connection with your heart, you have discovered the meaning of your life.

Your heart's passions are within you just like everything else. Everything outside of you is not actually real.

What do you mean not actually real? My job is not real? My house and all my money are not real? Poverty and suffering are not real?

They seem *real* in this human experience and

more so because we have created them. All these things outside of us are things we have produced in order to learn from them. We, *human-beings*, like to learn from tragedy, and incongruency. We create our own little tragedies in our everyday life and in the life of people around us. These tragedies extend to the community, the country, the planet. We have come to take for granted that our life's passage is meant to be a struggle, and that we are all alone. *My 'I' is a separate entity.* Which explains our feeling of loneliness, our sense of separateness and isolated beings.

It is now time to start relating in wholeness and fullness. Instead of creating tragedies for ourselves, let's create opportunities for full connection and complete reconnection.

> *"To read between the lines was easier*
> *than to follow the text."*
> Henry James [1843-1916]

Isn't this quote giving us the simple and easy way to our connectedness? In her book *The Bond — Connecting Through the Space Between Us*, Lynne McTaggart says: "What matters is not the isolated entity, but the space between things, the relationship of things." She goes on to say, " Every conflict that occurs — whether between husband and wife, social or racial groups, or nations — is resolved only when we can fully see and embrace the space — the bond — between us."

It is through our heart's passion {virtues} that we connect in the space between us.

Your *spirit-being* knows when something is actually real and when something is *meaningless*.

The next insight will take you right to the heart of what is *real*, therefore **Meaningful.**

CHAPTER TWELVE

Insight 8 – Meaningful

God did not create a meaningless world.
He did not create the situation which is disturbing you and so, it is not real.
Lesson 14
My thoughts do not mean anything
Lesson 10
A Course in Miracles
Foundation for Inner Peace
Helen Schucman

One needs to have been a student of ACM for many years to understand all of its 365 lessons. I would not call myself an expert on it, but some lessons stuck with me far more than others. Like lesson 10: My thoughts do not mean anything.

What do you mean "my thoughts do not mean anything"?

When you start searching for all the thoughts available to you, you will realize that they all come from the past or the future. That's why they do not mean anything.

You have the power to take each one of these thoughts and recognize that NOW they are meaningless.

**

Let's stop for a moment and look back at your day, your week, or even the past year. How many times have you stopped to be grateful and appreciative of all the things that you have accomplished that are meaningful? Do you see things for what they are? Do you look at life in the present time? Or do you look at it through your past experiences? Are you creating anything meaningful?

What does meaningful mean? You might think that something meaningful is different for everybody, right? Well, let me surprise you by saying no, it is not.

Mean-ing-ful is doing a simple action that leaves you feeling full – fulfilled. It is when giving and receiving becomes one and the same. It is when you share something that gives you that inner sense of higher purpose, and without expecting anything in return. Meaningful is having this elated fuzzy feeling after you have done a particular action. When you do or say something meaningful, it *all-ways* lifts your heart and uplifts the life of others.

Once you know this, you *all-ways* take the time to feel the implication of each action before doing them. You instantly and *all-ways* reflect on the purpose of the words you are about to share.

All-ways ask yourself: *What is the purpose of doing this or saying that? To whom is it significant? Is it meaningful to your essence, someone else's, or to your ego?*

Looking at our ego and admitting being in our ego is forever challenging for each one of us. This is why I am reserving a big section on *him/her/it* in Chapter Fourteen. Insight #10 will open the door to your Freedom. You will understand, perhaps for the first time, why *your thoughts do not mean anything*.

Before we do, let's take a look on how your beliefs create *meaningless* actions in your life.

Mean-ing-less is when you feel a sense of less or discontentedness after doing a particular action. These actions or those words were guided by your beliefs.

Your beliefs are just stories, and your stories are just beliefs. They are all one and the same. Stories [beliefs] that you have created or beliefs [stories] that you have learned from someone else. All *learned beliefs* are feeding your mind, and are all-ways managed by your Ego. Here's the Ego again! All beliefs are acquired or borrowed; they do not belong to you. You think they do, because you have them. You have them because you have accepted them as yours. Or simply, because you have created them yourself. Each and every one of us creates beliefs over and over again. Your beliefs about justice or integrity are probably different from mine. And my beliefs about justice and integrity will probably be different from my friends' beliefs.

Why is that? Because we borrow these beliefs from our parents, our teachers, our peers, our environment, our literature, even ourselves. Beliefs are just beliefs, just like an opinion is just an opinion. Imagine letting go of a lifetime of acquired beliefs to find yourself as light as a feather ready to soar in your greatness?

How does a belief become a belief? Where does it all start? Let's say you are a witness, along with a few neighbors, to a car accident in front of your house. As you observe the accident, you will react in a certain way based on the perception you just had. Your neighbors will do the same.

From that perception, you start creating a story, making one responsible for the accident and the other one the victim. Then you start believing that story. Simultaneously, your neighbors do the exact same thing. Based on their individual perception, they create their own story about the same exact accident, and go on believing that story. At the end, there are probably six different versions of the accident, even though only one accident happened.

Beliefs are the thoughts that you keep on replaying in your mind over and over again. Thoughts from the past and thoughts for the future. When you are in the immediate present, *the moment*, you have no thoughts. You are *in reality*.

Beliefs are thoughts that we don't question anymore.
Let's be with this one a little longer.
Your beliefs are thoughts that you don't question anymore.

They are filed in the box of the things you think you know, and you keep on adding to it. A belief is something that someone has given a definition to, a designation.

As soon as we give a "definition" to something, we create limits to what it is or to what it can be. A belief is always tainted. Always and "all-ways".

I know this might be difficult to grasp. So please remember my words from the beginning in **How to Read This Book.** Before you read further, take a moment to close your eyes and be with your emotions about this. Find your heart space. Please do it now.

From your heart space, go back to a moment in your life where you have done something for someone. It doesn't have to be anything grandiose. It could be something very simple such as helping an elderly lady stuck in the snow with her wheelchair. She turns around and looks at you with teary eyes filled with gratitude. How do you feel?

It could be having taken the time to tell an old friend, whom you haven't seen in a while, how much you appreciate her, and how much of a positive difference she has made in your life. How do you feel?

Or it could be you offered one of your dozen pairs of shoes to this homeless person on the street. He or she looks at you straight in the eyes, she doesn't say a word, just smiles, and you know that forever you are connected. How do you feel?

That's what I'm talking about. When you aim at living a meaningful life, your actions, your words do not come from your thoughts. They come from your heart. And when they do, you act on purpose — In *Meaningfulness.*

Are you starting to see how simple life really is? Do you feel connected to *your sense of purpose*?

When I embraced my vulnerability and surrendered, it took me to a place of deep peace. An unforeseen sanctuary.

Hand on the door handle, I turned the knob and entered…

CHAPTER THIRTEEN

Insight 9 - Emptiness

And here I am.

{is this page really empty?}

Suzanne Letourneau

*Emptiness which is conceptually liable to be mistaken
for sheer nothingness is in fact
the reservoir of infinite possibilities.*
D.T. Suzuki

*We cannot let another person into our hearts or minds
unless we empty ourselves. We can truly listen to him
or truly hear her only out of emptiness.*
M. Scott Peck

Great pieces for conversation wouldn't you say? "Emptiness as a human condition is known as a sense of generalized boredom, social alienation, and apathy. Feelings of emptiness often accompany depression, loneliness, despair, or other mental/emotional disorders. A sense of emptiness is also part of a natural process of grief as resulting of separation, death of a loved one, or other significant changes."

—*Wikipedia*

I certainly have experienced all of the feelings listed above, that's for sure. But not anymore.

When my Ego left me to my emptiness, I started feeling *fullness.* Fullness I had never felt before. Somehow "I" knew that **in my emptiness resides my fullness**.

Be clean, be pure, be empty because you will experience your own fullness. How can that be? Just imagine a blackboard filled with notes, formulas and drawings. It is so full of stuff that you need to erase them all before being able to write anything more.

It is a little similar with the emptiness process.

The empty canvas, the empty page in your book is full of possibilities. The place of creation where your fullness can be shared. The *social emptiness* is the one where you are filled with musts and shoulds, with darkness and blanks, and with separation and disconnectedness with yourself. The world we live in is characterized by fear, doubt, and division.

True emptiness is where serenity is. True emptiness is complete silence. In this silence all answers are given. It was after forty-nine days of total silence [meditation] that the Buddha found enlightenment. He had found the answers from within not from the outside.

Here's a simple meditation exercise: Try sitting alone in a quiet place thirty minutes a day and practice the listening of emptiness. Or you can choose to walk in silence for thirty minutes, stare at the sunset or the stars, or just sit in silence. Embracing your emptiness is not about creating isolation. It is about diving into the infinite source of life where all truth is and all answers are. It is about reconnecting to your source, your freedom. You can reconnect to your source when you work in your garden, when you cook, when you paint, etc. Whenever you do something or not, do something which brings you peace.

Freedom requires emptiness. Freedom lives in this place where there is no belief in connection to your thoughts, feelings, or experiences. Listen to your heart, be with your stillness because **in stillness resides your aliveness.**

The one and only real aliveness. The one that is connected to your source.

Soar With Vulnerability

"*Empty and still and full and alive*" is your natural state of being.

We live in a world where all that we are: love, freedom, authenticity, transparency, abundance, kindness, and so much more, has been cluttered with fear, judgment, shame, pride, destruction, disappointment and more. This is the world we have created. The world does not create what we are experiencing. We do that. Therefore if we had the power to create this world, we also have the power to recreate it. None of us has ever been power-less, only untruthful.

***

On that very same day, the day in the seminar, when I allowed my vulnerability to be seen and felt by everyone, I also felt an immense feeling of *defenselessness*. After putting the microphone down, people came over to me, thanking me for having had the courage to share that *secret* place. Something *they* would never be able to do, many said.

And there I was, in my truthfulness. It was not

courage or bravery. In order to have courage, you need to have a fear to confront or to conquer. But there was no more fear that I had not faced or experienced already. I was left with this huge feeling of defenselessness. Something really hard to describe as there's nothing quite like it.

Since that moment, before I do anything, I always reconnect to that particular place and feeling. When I feel that I am moving away from that serene place, or that my next action is taking me further from that peace and freedom, I consciously don't do it. I don't act on it, and I choose something else. I choose something that keeps me in my truth, not in my illusion.

I remain still and listen. Love is always there to guide me. In trust of *Love*, I dive into the unknown of my emptiness. This is where I found and experienced **Freedom** for the first time.

Are you ready to jump into the unknown?

CHAPTER FOURTEEN

Insight 10 - Freedom

In a previous insight I mentioned the *security of the unknown*. I will soon explain. But first, let's take a look at this *cliché* phrase: *afraid of the unknown*.

It never made sense to me. How can you be afraid of the unknown if you don't know it? How can you be afraid of something you do not know? We are only afraid of what we know, afraid of what we have experienced before. Or afraid of what our imagination congers up that *might be*. Even more, we are fearful of things that others have experienced. Fearful of what our parents or peers have told us to be afraid of.

One of the best examples I can give you on this is when I went skydiving for the first time. I had no fear whatsoever, only excitement. I did not have any previous experience to base my thoughts about it on. I had no one in my close environment who had experienced it, therefore no one to transfer their fear to me. I had an open heart and an open mind to the experience of it.

From the moment I jumped I had a smile glued to my face until I landed. And even then I could not take this smile of excitement off my face.

Shortly after, I learned that one of the other guys who jumped just before me froze up and forgot to pull his parachute rip cord. Wow! Thank God, we were doing a Progressive Free Fall jump. That's when you jump with two in-air interactive instructors.

You *free fall* for about 45 to 60 seconds then you have to pull your chute. You are responsible for all the required steps, as if you were on your own. The instructors are only there to assist. They check

Soar With Vulnerability

every move you make and if you forget anything they do it for you. In this case, they had to pull the chute for him.

The second time I went skydiving, already I had acquired a sense of fear. On this jump there were no instructors holding on to me, watching my every move. I was sitting by the open door of the small aircraft getting ready to jump, and I thought, *What are you doing here? You could end up hurting yourself. Maybe even die.* The fearful thoughts kept on circulating in my head, gluing me to the floor.

And then of course, I remembered that this was why I was there in the first place. To experience the thrill of skydiving. Once I overcame those limiting thoughts, I flung myself out on the wing, flapping like a flag in the wind for a few seconds, and then I calmly let go.

One thousand one, one thousand two, one thousand…time to pull my chute. *Where is it? Did it open?* I looked up. *There it is*! And there I was floating between heaven and earth, in awe of all the beauty. And only then did I fully relax into the exhilarating joy of that experience.

So why was I afraid the second time around?

Because I already had a preconceived idea of what *could* happen. A *belief* based on someone else's past experience. After all, I could forget to open my chute like the other guy had.

***

The *security of the known* is the playground you have created for yourself. It was fashioned on past events and experiences. You have created this comfort zone, where there is no risk, no danger. It is your limited knowing. In actuality, this comfort zone only creates boundaries for yourself.

The *security of the unknown* is the greatest and most exciting playground. It is the one that has been given to all of us in its absolute. When you engage into that playground, being open to the different *swings and slides*, it creates different and stimulating experiences for expansion. Expansion to your ultimate place of knowing. When you are in that place, all answers come to you like little stars falling from the sky. Magically *you* know. *You* just know. And *you* is not you. *You* are the answers.

Knowing is your natural state. *Knowing is you*. The unknown takes you back to who you are, without the Ego. Nevertheless, the Ego is somehow always part of us, like a faithful companion.

> *Ego is simply an idea of who you are*
> *that you carry around with you.*
> Wayne Dyer

Just an idea? Ideas come and go all the time. Why not this one? Why do we carry this one?

That day when I suddenly felt that something had died inside, leaving me with this wonderful sense of freedom, I did not understand what it was right away. But today I can tell you. It was my ego that had just diffused.

The ego is the so-called "social" friend. The friend that confuses everything, even the reality of who we really are. It is a stubbornness of the ego to imprison you in this projected comfort zone where the true messages are filtered and blocked. The purpose of this is only to suit the hungry and insatiable ego.

When you let go of the ego, the beliefs let go of you, and a whole new world of possibilities open up. You are open, you are curious. The purpose of the "letting go" is to regain the clarity and certainty of your heart — your spirit heart. And in order to find this place again, you need to be present. Present in the moment. Part of being free is to be present.

> *Freedom is the will to be responsible to ourselves*
> Friedrich Nietzsche

Your ego, once again, is always there somewhere, part of your life. To acknowledge the presence of your ego without judgment is also part of your life's experience. It is your *response-ability* for freedom.

I now acknowledge my ego with curiosity. I am conscious of his fear and I forgive him for his confusion. I ask myself: What is the lesson I need to learn today, for my ego to show up so unexpectedly? What is he here to show me?

When I make a shift into conscious awareness, I can unresponsively watch before making my soul choice.

The ego, along with all the fears it brings, is not your enemy. It is only what you do with the thoughts you have about the fears it brings. Fears

Soar With Vulnerability

such as anger, judgment, resentment, envy, etc.

A simple exercise: Next time you find yourself angry, or when you are judging others, ask yourself: "**What am I afraid of?**" And take a moment to be with the answer thoroughly and honestly.

Somebody cuts inside the line in front of you at the supermarket. *Who does she think she is? I have been waiting for the past fifteen minutes to check out. She has no right. She needs to get in line at the back like everybody else.* And now you are angry! **What am I afraid of?**

And this happens all the time. On the road while driving in traffic, at the airport check-in, at the bus stop, at concerts, at the movies, etc,. Actually, it has just happened to me the other day. While in line at the pharmacy, when it was my turn, a lady cut right in front of me, as if her long-winded question for the pharmacist took precedence over everything else.

When it happened I chose not to get angry. I decided to practice what I speak. I became a witness. People behind me looked at me and waited for my reaction.

I did nothing except to smile and be loving. Some of the other people in line raised their voices, demanding that this lady had to go to the back of the line. Others who had already been in line and were now sitting down, waiting for their names to be called, and judgmentally pointed their fingers at the lady. And others just stood there shaking their heads.

The clerk quickly answered her question, then apologized to everyone for the lady, and the day went on.

So why are you angry, really? What are you afraid of? That she is going to be out of the store 15 minutes before you? That this will make you late for an appointment? That she was audacious enough to do it? Or that you feel cheated or deprived of something?

Freedom is the will to be response-able to ourselves, response-able for our thoughts, for our feelings. It is to be accountable for our beliefs, our fears, and our limitations.

If it is the circumstance that causes our feelings, the feelings would be the same all around, wouldn't you think? But that is rarely the case. The emotional response is different for each one of us, because our reaction has nothing to do with what happened. It is about what we are *telling ourselves* about what happened.

Therefore it is our thoughts that generate our emotional response, not the external circumstance. External events are triggers, nothing more; they are not the cause of our emotional state.

What about anger? What about guilt, resentment, judgment, jealousy, and the like? If our thoughts *unconsciously* generate our emotional responses, could we say that each one of these feelings is simply an *unconscious* "reaction"? Or what I like to call it, an *action-reaction* action. Let me explain. Have you ever found yourself in a situation where for no apparent reason, this person starts yelling at you, calling you names, verbally attacking you? Seconds later, you find yourself doing the exact same thing back at her. Later on, you don't even remember how it all started.

It all-ways starts with a *perception*. We live in a world of perceptions. Therefore, we are reacting in action of our perception, of our judgment. This world of perception wants to have more clarity and more attention. Perhaps it is a way for the ego to bring us to see the real thing?

I will talk more about the ego's fears, or non-fear, at the end of the book, where you will learn to use a simple but powerful tool: **The Ego Releasing Chart**; it will help you see both sides of each and every fear, and show you how to use it for your positive growth.

To *be* your freedom, to live your freedom, start living your uniqueness versus your personality. When your ego is present, YOU are not there. When the ego is gone, YOU are there. Take notice when your ego is there, and be even more present.

When my ego let go of me that day at the seminar, it was because I was not working for him anymore. He was not winning, and he was not shining. He probably got tired of being ignored and left me to my emptiness. Ha! Ha! Ha! I am **Alive**.

CHAPTER FIFTEEN

Insight 11 - Alive & Soaring

Life is without meaning. You bring the meaning to it.
The meaning of life is whatever you ascribe it to be.
Being alive is the meaning.
Joseph Campbell

So many of us take our life for granted. And not only that, we often have difficulty being grateful for our family, our friends, our health, and our blessings. It is not until they are taken away from us that we start appreciating them.

Have you ever lost your eyesight for a short period of time? Or perhaps broken a leg? Have you been ignoring a family member out of unforgiveness for something that happened in the past? Have you been ignoring your own calling? Why do we always need to hit rock bottom before waking up to what is really meaningful in our life?

Suzanne Letourneau

**There is no greater feeling than the one of being alive because,
being alive is the meaning.**

At the very beginning of this book I shared with you how lifeless I was for many years, and how I doubted that there was anything still alive inside of me. Today, I am truly alive. What's more I can feel my aliveness. And that is truly a miracle.

It is a miracle because being numb is like being indifferent to the meaning of life; you cannot feel anything. And now, I feel and am more alive than ever.

As I am completing this book we are in the middle of *The Shift*. Wherever we are on the planet, we all feel it. We feel time moving faster, we feel agitated, more sensitive, more questioning. We all feel that something is happening, but we are not too sure of what it is.

Is it the end of the world? Is it the end of our world? Is it the end of humanity as we know it?

What is *The Shift?* Barbara Marx Hubbard considers it to be an expansion of consciousness when man will step into an evolutionary jump toward the emergence of a new species, a new being that is multidimensional, possessing expanded capacities for empathy, understanding and enlightenment. This new being, the *Universal Human*, she suggests, is the new humanity that will arrive because [man] will reach critical mass for this human by 2012. You can read more about it in her book *Emergence – The Shift from Ego to Essence*.

Does anybody know what's actually going on? Have the scientists identified the phenomena? I surely don't know what is really going on. All I am certain of is that from the moment I started living the eleven insights one by one in the order of this book, beautiful things started happening in my life. The first four insights are really the secrets in living your life in Conscious Awareness. That is because YOU are the Awareness in each and every moment.

I do trust we are in a destabilization phase for a higher expansion of who we are in reality. Furthermore, paying attention to your thoughts, and being aware of your emotions, is critical.

It is now time to have your ego work *for* you, the same way I have my ego work for me. Here's how it goes. Ask your ego to have its fears — hate, anger, worry, resentment, manipulation, control, etc. — be known to you, right out in the open. Without judgments, allow for these fears to be released and reintegrated as lessons learned. This could take the form of a new adventure that challenges your sense of security. Either a spiritual journey — discovering a new philosophy or a new faith — a new activity that takes you out of your comfort zone, and will result in a new sense of empowerment of the unknown.

Don't get caught up in its fears – greed, blame, judgment, jealousy and confusion. When you do so, it automatically lowers your energy and provides power for chaos, and those who feed off it.

Have you ever entered a room where the level of energy is extremely low and negative, due to unmeaningful thoughts and actions happening in that room? We all have experienced it at some time and, will experience it again.

There is definitely more challenges, traumas, and dis-ease that will surface. Look at them as opportunities for learning and growth. The big difference now is that you have tools. You have

Soar With Vulnerability

Eleven Powerful Insights that will help you along the way.

You might have heard of the book *The Law of Attraction* by Esther and Jerry Hicks? There are multiple versions of it. It is about this new discovered change in man's ability to *manifest intention.*

My intention is to BE ALIVE and FEEL ALIVE.

My intention is to live a true **meaningful** life in conscious awareness.

My mission is to stay in my spirit heart, to stay in *LOVE*
Our True essence.

It is time for each and every one of us to truly be alive and soar to our greatness!

Please join me!

The Ego Releasing Chart

Earlier I stated that the Ego can have its benefits. How can the Ego be used to learn and grow, versus hurting and destroying yourself and others?

You are either in *Fear* or in *Love*. You are either in Ego or in your Higher Consciousness. It is up to you to be attentive of *when and where you are, when you are there*. Without any judgments, just be aware and embrace the moment of this particular energy.

If it is a loving energy you will willingly and naturally share it with everyone around you. Everyone will be open to receive your sharing of love and happiness. Even if they have feelings of fear themselves. *Love transcends all.* You see, *Fear* and *Love*, are the two biggest contestants in this physical life.

*Love is your natural state of essence,
and is always challenged
with your outer state of being.*

I have created this simple **Ego Releasing Chart** as a tool to help you recognize when you are living in fear. For each fear is a reminder of your *human-essence*. Each fear brings along an opportunity to reconnect to your *soul-essence* and, one of humility for the ego. Whenever you find yourself in any of the following Emotion-Reaction situations, know that you are in *Ego Fear*.

Once again, there is nothing wrong with that, as long as you can see it, be with it, recognize it, and transform it.

We all try to cover our fears. They are always there beneath the surface, with the ego. **The only way you can be without fear, is to accept your fear when it is present.** Once you accept it and connect with it, it has no more reason to make you fearful. It simply brings you a different perspective for you to reflect on. And that goes for all the Emotion-Reaction episodes that you experience each and every day of your life.

Furthermore, knowing how to understand your emotional state of mind as an indication of the state of your consciousness is a great advantage. Our physical minds and bodies are having great difficulty communicating to each other. We need to tap in to our "inner" mind; the untainted one where all knowledge and understanding resides.

EGO'S FEAR LIST

Anger

Caused by both internal and external events, anger is internal when you start believing your negative thoughts. External is when you believe you need to defend yourself, that you need to respond to some external threats. Your heart rate goes up, and so does your energy.

Therefore, whenever you find yourself in anger, have your anger work for you. Use your anger for a positive outcome versus a negative one. Do one of your favorite physical activities. This could be a great workout at the gym, a run in the country — do an extra mile farther than you usually do. It could be to plant the big trees that you always wanted to, or just to dance wildly to your favorite music at maximum volume, until your feet cannot do another step.

Do something productive. Does your wardrobe need spring cleaning, even if it's not spring? Organize your basement or even your garage which you have been postponing for so long. Or, cut some wood for next winter.

You will be surprised at how much you will have done in very little time, as anger gives you extra strength. Once this extra strength has been used to a point of exhaustion, the anger will have disappeared. You are now able to see clearly and make new decisions calmly and serenely.

One more tip, in order to see how *ridiculously ugly* you look when angry, step in front of the mirror and yell all that anger at the image you see looking back at you. Now, stop and feel. If the anger is still there, repeat the exercise. Repeat until you can look at yourself in the mirror and laugh.

MEDITATION: *I thank you, Anger, for being such a good Trainer.*

Anxiety

Unlike excitement, anxiety comes from not trusting, not living in the moment. When you feel anxious, it is time to breathe all that you are, one breath at a time. Breathe in the life that you are — then exhale the fear that is suffocating you. Feel the love that you are — then release the doubts that are stopping you. Trust in you, the higher consciousness. You are not alone and never will be. It is time to listen.

Create a quiet and special place where you can just sit and listen. Listen to your favorite soft music, listen to the birds. Listen to the soft whisper of the wind, or simply listen in for your heartbeat. Feel! You are alive. What a great gift!

Be grateful, be happy, and be empty. Let all thoughts go. Breathe.

Have a long relaxing bubble bath, light some candles, and let yourself be transported on this soft fluffy cloud. Feel this precious moment. Breathe. Trust that all is good. Breathe.

Once you have released this *false* energy that anxiety gives you, the fear is gone.

MEDITATION: *I thank you, Anxiety, for being such a good Guide.*

Ashamed

Shame comes up when you are judging yourself based on your own values, the ones that you have formulated for yourself. Shame is also formed based on someone else's values. Shame is always about who you are. About who you think you are [worthless and insignificant] or about who you think you are not [great and precious]. No matter what, it is all-ways based on some values. These values are always mind created and therefore are at all times making someone right and someone wrong. That's what the mind does.

The values [virtues] that are in your heart, in your higher consciousness are never judgmental. They are part of who you are, part of your wholesomeness.

When you feel ashamed, make sure you move

into your *conscious awareness* state, so you can feel without judging, without condemning, without accusing. See the shame, feel the shame, accept the shame and as you do, the shame will become the healer that will guide you on the path of true and pure values — your virtues. When your virtues are applied in complete integrity, they are disconnected from your beliefs. Your virtues are innate; your values are learned, conditioned. Once you have released the "mind" values, the shame disappears, the fear is gone.

MEDITATION: *I thank you, Shame, for being such a good Healer.*

Betrayed - Cheated – Deceived

One or all of these three come up when you have put your trust in someone who has exposed you, putting you in a place of *helplessness*. So you feel betrayed, cheated, and deceived.

You can only feel betrayed, cheated, or deceived when you have placed your trust where trust is disposable. It is not by trusting others or even yourself that you will gain the reassurance.

It is in putting your trust in your inner strength; the strength of your source within you, which is there for you in all situations and every part of any situation.

In this source of love you trust. Love is your blissful trust.

Love is what you are, love is what you are here for, and what you are here to learn. This phrase might seem like it is contradicting itself. But let's read it backwards and you will feel how nicely it sits in your whole being.

Love is what you are here to learn, love is what you are here for, and love is what you are! Once you have released the "illusion" or need for outside trust, the betrayal, the deception disappears. The fear is gone.

MEDITATION: *I thank you, Illusion, for being such a good Wizard.*

Soar With Vulnerability

Concerned - Confused

When confusion or concern arises, it is because you are in doubt about who you are, confused about joy and pain, about love and fear. And the ONLY way out of another erroneous belief is to accept that you do not have to decide or do anything. Just BE.

Everything that has been given to you, confusion, concern and all, came with the blessing from the higher source. Your spurious decision making, which is enviously guarded by the ego, will never achieve what the higher source has in store for you.

Your higher consciousness will lead you and guide you out of the confusion that you yourself have created. BE still. Embrace your emptiness. BE alive.

Once you have released the "spurious decision making", the confusion disappears, the fear is gone.

MEDITATION: *I thank you, Spurious Decision Making, for being such a good Teacher.*

Defeated

Feeling defeat is thinking that you have failed at something.

Remember that failure is an event, not a person.
(Zig Ziglar)

The only failure in life is the failure to try.
(Unknown)

There are no failures – just experiences and your reactions to them.
(Tom Krause)

Failure is never about you. It is about something that happened, or something that is happening. Something that is outside of you; in the *reality* of your illusion. Whenever you start feeling like you have failed, look at the experience that is offered to you. Take the time to detach yourself from the whole event and pretend that this particular situation is happening to someone else. Become the witness. What would you tell them?

Soar With Vulnerability

When you feel like a failure you become a victim in loss. A victim all-ways makes somebody wrong. With every loss you have, you receive a much bigger win.

Once you can see the win, the loss is gone.

MEDITATION: *I thank you, Defeat, for being such a good Liberator.*

Dis-appointed

You can only be disappointed when you live in expectations. Therefore, do your best from your heart and have confidence. Whatever happens IS exactly what is supposed to be. We each have a unique purpose in life. Our purpose was appointed to each and every one of us with the highest good of all at heart. There is no point fighting it. The Universe knows exactly what you need and when you need it. Even though there are no needs to have.

Take comfort in each disappointment. For each setback is there to remind you that the Universe has something better and bigger in store for you.

Everything happens in divine order. When you let go of the misfortune, the miracle happens.

MEDITATION: *I thank you, Setback, for being such a good Clairvoyant.*

Dis-couraged

This occurs when you have lost track of your WHY. When you are living your WHY, *never* are you without courage. You're WHY, moves mountains. Your WHY is what keeps the fire burning. The WHY is the vision at the end of the tunnel. Your WHY is in direct connection with your *core-essence*. Let go of the *what* and the *how*. Keep the focus on your WHY and you'll never be alone. You will never be dis-connected.

MEDITATION: *I thank you, Dis-couragement, for being such a good Enlightenment.*

Soar With Vulnerability

Dis-gusted

You are being in judgment. You have created separation with the Oneness that we are. You see the object of disgust outside of yourself. Take this opportunity to change your thoughts about what is disturbing you in this situation. Make this an occasion to appreciate the repulsive object. When you let go of the critical thoughts, the judgment disappears. When you let go of hostility, gratitude can be expressed.

MEDITATION: *I thank you, Separation, for being such a good Unifier.*

Embarrassed

You are in judgment of yourself. The self that you think you ought to be. Embarrassed is when you are *self-conscious* instead of being *consciously conscious*. Through sincere awareness you will see that everything that you are self-conscious about has nothing to do with you. All the thoughts and ideas that you have about yourself are just that —

thoughts and ideas. It has no core, no essence. Your true self has no ties to the thoughts or ideas that the mind has.

Let go of the conscious self and open the door to being consciously conscious. Start playing freely in the comfort of your awareness of awareness.

MEDITATION: *I thank you, Self-Consciousness, for being such a good Dreamer.*

Empty

A great opportunity to find your fullness.

We shape clay into a pot, but it is the emptiness inside that holds whatever we want.
Lao Tsu

We are never empty, as we are everything there is. It is only our human-essence that occasionally feels empty. And this happens only when we have lost our life's purpose. You are consciousness in action.

Close your eyes. Empty your mind of all

thoughts and be completely still. Breathe. Breathe and receive. In that emptiness and that stillness you still exist. You are existence without thoughts, concepts or ideas. Tune in into your true nature and be on your way to fullness.

MEDITATION: *I thank you, Emptiness, for being such a good Receiver.*

Exhausted - Frustrated

It is a time to introspect. Are you going against the current of your life? If you feel that everything is more like a fight instead of being a gentle flow, perhaps it is time to take a step aside. Try helping someone who needs even more help than you do. We are in an era of collaboration and co-creation. Encouraging and supporting someone in greater need will make your needs seem meaningless.

MEDITATION: *I thank you, Frustration, for being such a good Collaborator.*

Grief

A time to reflect and reconnect to your Source. You body is a vehicle for experiences — for the Source, and to the Source.

Someone said: *There is grief to help us cope, there is God to give us hope.*

Painful thoughts and strange feelings are one and the same in time of grief.

Remember my earlier admonition: *Pain is a gift when we choose to accept that it is there for a particular teaching for ourselves or others.*

Pain is tremendously present in time of grief — for the loss of a loved one, loss of a cherished dream, loss of your dear pet, loss of anything that was taken from you. How can it be a gift?

Once again, in the sharing of your pain the lesson will manifest itself. The Universe sends you experiences that the Source needs to experience — with you and within you. Embrace the grief and peace will settle in.

MEDITATION: *I thank you, Grief, for being such a good Mentor.*

Soar With Vulnerability

Guilty

Never is guilt about you. It is about something you did. So here you are judging yourself once again. What you do is not who you are. It is only the results of your thoughts. It is the lack of inspiration.

Inspiration is directly connected to the Source. It is an action to inspire. Therefore to elevate, not to lower. When you are feeling guilty, take response-ability for your actions. Know that you have chosen to say or do something meaningless. Take a deep breath.

Life is in the moment. Not of the past or the future. Now is the time to do something meaningful.

MEDITATION: *I thank you, Guilt, for being such a good Listener.*

Heartbroken

You are depending on someone else for your happiness.

Suzanne Letourneau

*It is not easy to find happiness in ourselves,
and it is not possible to find it elsewhere.*

Agnes Repplier

Your heart can only be broken when you think you are incomplete. When you think that you need that person or that something to be happy. It is all part of the illusion. For too many years now, society has used the expression "better half", when talking about a person's partner in life. No one is half completed. We are whole, part of a whole. If you let go of the illusion of separation, you will never be heartbroken ever again. Wholeness is what you are.

MEDITATION: *I thank you, Broken heart, for Being such a good Counselor.*

Helpless [help-less]

Remember Insight # 8? Meaningless versus meaningful. Acting out of beliefs instead of acting from the heart. *Help-less*: You are without help. It is when you have forgotten your true power. You have unconsciously cut off the string connecting you to your inner [virtue] heart.

You are not in charge. Something much bigger is. Appreciate the moment of not having to be in command. You have nothing to control. All is good. Breathe. Let go. Listen. Breathe. Receive your new assignment.

MEDITATION: *I thank you, Helplessness, for being such a good Advisor.*

Humiliated

Humiliation occurs when you are giving outside value to an outside opinion. It is when you believe your own perceptions. Humil*iation* is a feeling. Humil*ity* is being. Can you feel how humility reunites, and how humiliation divides? Nothing outside of you is meaningful. Nothing can disrespect YOU – only the false self — the ego constantly creates that. You are born without ego. The ego comes from the outside world. Therefore it is meaningless.

The real can be known only through the false, said Osho. Hence you want to go through the ego self in order to find and live your truth. Going through the ego is a human-essence process, a social exercise. We all have to experience it. It is part of the illusionary reality.

Live your humbleness, for it is a heart virtue. Leave the humiliations to the stories people have of you. Breathe. You are humble, you are love spirit.

MEDITATION: *I thank you, Humiliation, for being such a good Reflector.*

***

As you probably have realized by now, *each and every fear* is Ego based. The Ego creates it all. I could have chosen to list all of the fears that exist, and break them down to the source. Quite a lengthy process — and an unnecessary one. You see, the source of fear is always the same. It is *all-ways* produced by the *Ego-Self*.

How about the psychological fears, such as fear of flying? Same. It is based on a bad experience, or the bad experience of someone else. Then the negative thoughts about *the experience, amplifies to a point of no return.*

How about the fear of losing someone you love, through sickness or even death? Same. Your fear is not about them, it is about you; your Ego-Self that is scared of being alone. The Self that believes in separation.

I invite you to continue reading down the Ego Releasing Chart. Dive into the opportunity to fully participate in releasing any or all ego experiences that are now present in your life. Breaking down each fear will help you find peace and serenity. I encourage you to use each one of the meditations to solidify the release you just made and keep on practicing to prevent any ego experiences that might crop up in the future. When Fear is present Love is submerged. When Love surfaces Fear dissolves.

Hurt — Pain

Is Emotional pain a result of physical pain? Or is the bodily pain an outcome of the emotion? I found that they are closely intertwined and work in a vicious cycle. Therefore you need to understand the source of the pain in order to start the healing process. Take a moment to revisit Chapter Seven, Insight 3.

Whenever pain is present, know that it is there to teach you something. It is an opportunity for expansion. You need to put your attention beyond the experience of the pain. When pain is coming from within, make sure you listen and welcome it. Feel it, cry, scream, live it, be it, then let go. Peace is waiting.

When pain is coming from outside, you know it is part of the reality of the illusion we are living on this planet. This too will pass. Allow, listen, and witness the communication progression. Find the true comfort in painfulness.

MEDITATION: *I thank you, Pain, for being such a good Cleanser.*

Impatient

This occurs when you are out of the moment. It is when you have stopped living in the NOW. Or when NOW doesn't seem to be sufficient anymore. Or you feel like you are running out of time.

Soar With Vulnerability

Time does not really exist. There is no past and no future. There is only NOW in the moment.

Learn from the space between each moment and gradually you will find the understanding of *reality*.

Choose to be consciously aware of each and every moment. Become aware of all thoughts until there are no more thoughts. You have returned to the place where there is no time, no limitation.

MEDITATION: *I thank you, Impatience, for being such a great Anchor.*

Loss

You refuse to see the awakening gift sent by the Divine force. As you are focused on playing the actor's part in your movie, you forget that you also have the producer's role at hand. The producer sees the whole picture.

It is time for you to wear both hats at all times. Giving and receiving are one and the same, loss and gain are a whole on its own. It cannot be separated.

What you *perceive* to have lost was planned a long time ago, in order to bring you to where you are now. You would not be the person that you are today without having experienced all these perceived losses.

MEDITATION: *I thank you, Loss, for being such a great Gift.*

Rage

When you are in rage, you are blocking the true flow of life. Rage is a long-term anger that you have been holding back. Have you ever heard the expression: *I don't know what happened. I just saw red?* Your anger is now uncontrollable. The options were there, you had the choice — before.

Rage will give you a false feeling of control offsetting the feeling of incompetency and the perceived outside source of abuse. In order to completely heal rage, it needs to express itself. It needs to explode in tears. It needs to inhale love. It is time to center yourself and feel the feeling.

Whether the rage is directed toward yourself or

toward someone else, it is time to connect with the trigger of this rage. Remember, the seed of rage is anger. Thoughts are the foundation of your anger. And anger is meant to be *healthily* expressed (see Anger), understood, and then let go of.

MEDITATION: *I thank you, Rage, for showing me Healthy Anger.*

Resentment — Bitterness

Resentment settles in when long-standing forgiveness hasn't been offered. This forgiveness needs to be offered in love; for yourself and others.

Resentment is re-sending an emotion that you are re-living from the past. This emotion has created and continues to breed separation. The emotion was fed by a fearful thought of lack and deception. When that happens you are without a doubt living a feeling of disconnection.

In *a resentful* separation we rarely see others with less than we have. We generally choose to see them with a lot more than we have.

Without the separation, we are ONE. Therefore

what is yours is mine and what is mine is yours. It is OURS. None of us can be without it. We are the *Heart*.

MEDITATION: *I thank you Bitterness, for reminding me of my Sweetness.*

Sad

As opposed to happiness, sadness often comes unexpectedly and sometimes without apparent reason. It floats slowly toward your heart until your whole heart is covered; just like the sun is wrapped in heavy clouds before a storm.

And then the rainstorm starts. You are now crying for love instead of giving love. How can you cry for love when you are LOVE? You have merely forgotten that behind those thick black clouds, the sun [love] is still there shining to its maximum.

No matter what the weather might be.

Therefore Love is all-ways there. *Get on the plane and fly over these clouds* and let the sun warm and dry your tears. You are loved, as you are Love.

Soar With Vulnerability

MEDITATION: *I thank you Sadness, for showing rain and sun as the reality of One.*

Scared — Fearful

There is nothing to fear but fear itself.
Franklin D. Roosevelt

The most powerful enemy of fear is Love. And once again, love is what you are.

Love is what you are here for. When you are in fear, you are ignoring your true self.

When you are angry, ask yourself, *What am I afraid of?*

When you are afraid ask, *What other assignment do you have for me?* And…Trust!

You are only a small grain in the sand that gets lifted up through the limitless unity of love. It is time to rise above this mis-trust and move on.

MEDITATION: *I thank you, Fear, for Lifting me! Ha! Ha!*

Selfish [self-ish]

What is Self? *You can only give but to yourself as we are all connected as one.* When feeling the need to be *self-ish* you are looking at things from a separation and a lack point of view. The small self is present and YOU are not.

Abundance is within you and around you — limitless. Abundance is something you simply feel.

MEDITATION: *I thank you, Selfishness, to open the door to my Gratitude.*

***

Before we go into the last string of *fear* words, let's look at the suffix "un".

Isn't it interesting how powerfully this suffix can change a word's meaning?

"Un" can transform a positive word into a negative one and vice versa: unable, unafraid, unappreciative, etc. Therefore for each of the negative words starting with "un", replace the "un" with "Om".

"Om" is a mantra, an intonation which transcends all barriers. "Om" the symbol represents both the *un-manifested* and the *manifested* aspects of Life. It is said to be the planet's primordial vibration. When humming or chanting the word "Om", its resonance will reconnect you with your true soul essence. Let's try it.

For each of the following words, take the time to hum or chant the new "Om' word at least 3 times.

When in doubt tell the truth.
Mark Twain

When in doubt, don't.
Benjamin Franklin

Un-certain *(Om-certain)*

The Ego wants to confuse you. When you live your WHY's — your purpose in life — you are all-ways certain. This doesn't mean that you won't have any challenging moments or choices to make. It only means that the Universe has provided you with an extra opportunity for you to get closer to your passion, your *Om-certain.*

You all-ways have the choice. The option to act

or not to act, to think or not to think, and to be or not to be. Every challenging moment is an opportunity for growth — ascension.

MEDITATION: *I thank you, Uncertainty, for guiding my Ascension.*

Un-appreciated — Un-worthy (*Om-appreciated — Om-worthy*)

Your human-essence feels unloved. But Love is what you are.

Om-appreciated: Life, the Absolute, the Universe loves you, appreciates you. It is time to reflect upon your perfection. Do you remember the *Footprints in the Sand* poem? Here's a part of it:

...but I have noticed that during the most troublesome times in my life there is only one set of footprints.

"I don't understand why in times when I needed you most, you should leave me."

The Lord replied, "My precious, precious child, I love you and I would never, never leave you.

During your times of trial and suffering, when you saw only one set of footprints, it was then that I carried you."

Whenever you feel un-appreciated, un-loved, know that LOVE itself is carrying you.

MEDITATION: *I thank you, Unworthiness, for showing me Love's Footprints.*

Un-motivated *(Om-motivated)*

You are ignoring your inspiration. You are not in alignment with your purpose. *Om-motivated*: Let the inspiration that you are guide you to your purpose. Motivation doesn't come from the outside world. This too, is part of the illusion.

Motivation is natural and effortless when the true inspiration that you are flows through you.

MEDITATION: *I thank you, Inspiration, for removing the Illusion.*

Un-sure *(Om-sure)*

You have forgotten the wis-d-*Om* of meaningfulness. When you do or say something meaningful it *all-ways* lifts your heart. All-ways choose the opportunity that gives you that fuzzy feeling of connectedness. *Om-sure* — Life, Love is meaning-full.

Therefore, direct your attention to the purpose of each thing. Every thing and any thing has its purpose. Purpose is meaning unlimited.

MEDITATION: *I thank you, Hesitation, for offering Endless Vision.*

Victimized

You continuously choose to believe your thoughts. You have made yourself a subject of deception, for something that is happening outside yourself.

Remember, your thoughts are NEVER neutral and nothing outside your self is meaning-full. When you remove yourself from the emotions that your thoughts are creating, you liberate yourself from all outside power. You only become a victim when you allow it. Which one will you choose?

MEDITATION: *I thank you, Vulnerability, for bringing my Liberation.*

***

*Only when we are brave enough to explore
the darkness will we discover
the infinite power of our light*

The Gifts of Imperfection

Brené Brown, Ph.D., L.M.S.W

Writing this book and even more, finishing it, is a life adventure on its own. One needs to be prepared to go beyond their comfort zone and be prepared to share some of their darker side with the world. Moving out from a world of duality, we want to understand both sides in order to move forward in collaboration and co-creation.

It will eventually make sense that being victimized or unvictimized has no distinction. No difference is made between vulnerability and invulnerability; it is one and the same. It is what we **choose to ignore** as a joint humanity.

Our darkness needs our light as our light needs our darkness.

It is our balance in this experiential world.

ACKNOWLEDGMENTS

Thank you Cliff Carle, my editor, for your eagle eyes in catching all of my grammar mistakes and keeping me on track with my message. Thank you for seeing early on, how this book can transform lives. http://www.cliffcarle.com/

Thank you Tunde Nyarfadi-Duncan from TNy Photography for my natural head portrait.
http://tnyphotography.ca/Tunde/Index.html

Thank you Elaine Lanmon for the layout design of the book as well as the engaging book cover. Thank you for making the time in the middle of your move to work on this project.

I would like to also give a big thank you to all who have helped me without knowing it, throughout my life. I have learned so much from each and every one of you: Marianne Williamson, Louise

Suzanne Letourneau

Hay, Eckhart Tolle, Neale Donald Wash, Brendon Burchard, Paul Ferrini, Lynne Mc Taggart, Greg Habstritt, Napoleon Hill, Janet Bray Attwood, Alan Cohen, Larry Dossey, Brian Weiss, Barbara De Angelis, Dr. Joe Vitale and so many more.

Thank you to my unstoppable colleagues Colleen Lindberg, Jennifer Ettinger, Susan Plantamura, Sandra Lake, Jennifer Fisher, Dagmar Schoenrock, Michelle Peavy, Leslie Rivas Taranto for your understanding and encouragement.

Thank you to my dear and close friends Annemarie Debont, Dorine Lettinga, Veronica Albanese, Ed Kimmel for your unconditional love.

Thank you to my mother, Thérèse, my older sister Carole, my younger sister Gisèle, for being great teachers with your lives.

Thank you to Janet Bray-Attwood, Gerry Visca and Sean Patrick Simpson for the endorsement on my book. I am honored by your kind words and grateful for your encouragement and support. Thank you so much.

Thank you to Stan, my partner in life for being as amazing as you are.

Soar With Vulnerability

ABOUT THE AUTHOR

Suzanne Letourneau was born and raised in Montreal, Quebec.

Her quest for a spiritual connection to all around her led to extensive travel and the experiencing of many cultures, religions and philosophies.

She is an entrepreneur at heart and has multiple career and business accomplishments to her credit. In addition to her careers as a Flight Attendant and personal trainer, she was also the founder of the award winning OraOxygen Airport Spa, the first of its kind in the world.

She has co-authored two books: *"Adventures in Manifesting — Health & Happiness"* and *"The Unstoppable Woman's Guide to Emotional Well-Being"*. Suzanne is a lively and enthusiastic speaker who facilitates from her heart & soul, <u>from the future backwards</u>, with stories that motivate and inspire.

When asked why she does what she does, her answer is simply: '**I exist to inspire others to truly**

experience life and live truthfully. Get Curious. Be Outrageous'. She challenges you to step out of your comfort zone to explore new possibilities.

Soar with Vulnerability is the first in a series of SOAR books. The SOAR movement includes workshops and seminars for individuals and companies, with such topics as 'Soar with Passion — *How to Live Fully, Get Rid of Your BUT and Engage in Your WHY*', 'Soar with Vulnerability — *No More Hiding: Embrace the Real You and Be Free* ' to name but a few.

When she is not working on a new project she loves to golf, dance, swim with wild dolphins in the open water, read, write and travel.

For more information on Suzanne Letourneau and her upcoming work, please visit:

www.suzanneletourneau.com

BIBLIOGRAPHY

E.R. Haas & Kent C. Madson, *Success on Purpose* 2007

Louise L. Hay, *Heal Your Body* 1978

Terry Cole-Whittaker, *What you think of me is none of my business* 1979

Napoleon Hill, *A year of Growing Rich* 1993

Barbara Marx Hubbard, *Emergence — The Shift from Ego to Essence* 2001

Simon Sinek, *Start with Why* 2009

Lynne McTaggart, *The Bond—* 2011

www.ingramcontent.com/pod-product-compliance
Lightning Source LLC
Chambersburg PA
CBHW032118090426
42743CB00007B/382